T0316609

Kinetic Beauty

Sport aesthetics is an important but often marginalized field in the philosophy of sport. *Kinetic Beauty* offers a comprehensive, principled, pluralist introduction to the philosophical aesthetics of sport.

The book tackles a wide variety of issues in the philosophical aesthetics of sport, proposing a five-level analysis that coordinates extant scholarship on the same conceptual map, reveals gaps in the literature, and motivates a fresh perspective on stubborn debates and novel topics in the field (for example, the aesthetic experience of athletes, aesthetic biases in sport, the paradox of sport fiction, and whether dance can be sport).

This is an excellent resource for professors and students in the philosophy of sport, sport aesthetics, general aesthetics, and the philosophy of art. It is also a fascinating read for those working in kinesiology, sport studies, philosophy, art, and aesthetics.

Jason Holt is Professor of Kinesiology at Acadia University, Canada.

Ethics and Sport

Series editors

Mike McNamee
University of Wales Swansea

Jim Parry
University of Leeds

The *Ethics and Sport* series aims to encourage critical reflection on the practice of sport, and to stimulate professional evaluation and development. Each volume explores new work relating to philosophical ethics and the social and cultural study of ethical issues. Each is different in scope, appeal, focus and treatment but a balance is sought between local and international focus, perennial and contemporary issues, level of audience, teaching and research application, and variety of practical concerns.

Recent titles include:

Sport, Ethics, and Neurophilosophy
Jeffrey Fry and Mike McNamee

Doping in Cycling
Interdisciplinary Perspectives
Edited by Bertrand Fincoeur, John Gleaves and Fabien Ohl

Sport and Spirituality
Edited by R. Scott Kretchmar and John B. White

The Philosophy of Football
Steffen Borge

Kinetic Beauty
The Philosophical Aesthetics of Sport
Jason Holt

Kinetic Beauty

The Philosophical Aesthetics
of Sport

Jason Holt

Routledge
Taylor & Francis Group

LONDON AND NEW YORK

First published 2020 by Routledge

2 Park Square, Milton Park, Abingdon, Oxon OX14 4RN
605 Third Avenue, New York, NY 10017

Routledge is an imprint of the Taylor & Francis Group, an informa business

First issued in paperback 2021

British Library Cataloguing-in-Publication Data
A catalogue record for this book is available from the British Library

Library of Congress Cataloging-in-Publication Data
A catalog record for this book has been requested

ISBN: 978-0-367-33532-8 (hbk)
ISBN: 978-1-03-217664-2 (pbk)
DOI: 10.4324/9780429320439

Typeset in Times New Roman
By Apex CoVantage, LLC

Contents

Acknowledgments

Thanks to colleagues who proved particularly encouraging and collaborative, notably Sylvia Burrow, Andrew Fenton, Larry Holt, William Irwin, Darren Kruisselbrink, John MacKinnon, Hans Maes, Letitia Meynell, Ira Newman, Robert Pitter, Bernie Wills, and Marisa Yeomans.

Thanks to everyone at Routledge, especially series editors Jim Parry and Mike McNamee, as well as Simon Whitmore and Rebecca Connor.

Thanks also to my parents, Alyce and (again) Larry Holt; my wife, Megan Haliburton; and the baristas at *Just Us* Wolfville, where most of this book was first drafted.

Chapter 9 first appeared as J. Holt (2017), 'Sport as Art, Dance as Sport', *Acta Universitatis Carolinae Kinanthropologica*, *53* (2): 138–45. Creative Commons Attribution License 4.0.

'Myron's *Discobolus*' (Figure 8.1; Wills 2019) was commissioned for this book. Thanks to Jean Wills for her artistry.

Introduction
Pregame

Despite its undeniable ugly side, sport can be a beautiful thing, even sub-lime, and that – from a philosophical perspective – is what this book is about: the aesthetics of sport. There is no doubt that sport in some form or other is appreciated by many people and in most cultures around the world. But when you look at what sport philosophers have had to say about values in sport, you may get the impression that it is moral and ethical values that predominate in this arena. Indeed, sport ethics is unquestionably the single largest part of sport philosophy, and this is reflected as much in the public interest as in academic ink spilled on such matters as the use of performance-enhancing drugs. Yet an important part of the value of sport resides in its beauty, which is multifaceted and well worth philosophers' attention both in its own right and as an example of what is sometimes called everyday aesthetics.[1] Though some philosophers have looked at sport from an aesthetic point of view, this approach remains a marginalized one in philosophical investigations of sport.

If you look at the sport aesthetics literature, you will note that much of it concerns issues delimited locally if not somewhat narrowly. On one hand are questions about the relationship between sport and art: whether sport *is* art and, to a lesser extent, representations of sport *in* art. On the other hand are questions about the relationship between sport and the aesthetic: aesthetic sports, where style points awarded by judges figure into the determination of outcomes, and how aesthetics arises in sport generally, even where such judgments are not relevant to who wins and who loses. Concerning the aesthetics of sport generally, different subtopics have been addressed including graceful movement, sport drama, creative style, game types and design norms, purism versus partisanship, and aesthetic–moral interaction. Each area constitutes a well-defined though more or less theoretically isolated scholarly domain.

Despite the insights in many of these areas, the scholarship has significant shortcomings. It is disjoint, incomplete, subtypical, and unresolved. To explain, I will tackle each point in turn. First, it is disjoint. There has been little concerted effort to illuminate relationships among these various areas, much less to provide a theoretical framework broad enough to orient the results of this research in the same conceptual landscape. Second, it is incomplete. Several useful concerns have not been discussed by sport philosophers, such as not just aesthetic judgment in general but aesthetic *bias* in particular. Third, it is subtypical. Most research concerns *examples* of the types of phenomena we are interested in rather than the *types* themselves. Sport philosophers have offered accounts of what makes movement graceful, for instance, but only to the neglect of other aesthetic properties such as expressiveness. Fourth, it is unresolved. Even within each pocket of scholarship many debates seem, if not at a standstill, ongoing at a slow pace. This is not atypical of philosophy, yet many of these debates could probably benefit from fresh approaches, which is also not atypical of philosophy. I will proceed on the assumption that making progress on many of these debates will depend on formulating a broad theoretical framework that helps illuminate relationships among pockets of scholarship, identify gaps in the literature, and reveal unexplored lines of inquiry in approaching sport from an aesthetic point of view.

The principal purpose of this book is to provide a philosophical aesthetics of sport in the broadest sense. The approach will be systematic, employing appropriate levels of contextualism and pluralism in addressing specific questions and broad concerns about the aesthetic properties of sport, the nature of aesthetic sports, and the relationships between sport and art. My hope is to raise both the profile of, and scholarly interest in, the philosophical aesthetics of sport.

There is, however, one major hurdle to clear first: skepticism about the very idea of sport aesthetics. In its most trenchant form, Paul Ziff (1974: 93) puts it thus: 'Research devoted to the aesthetics of sport can accomplish nothing'. His reasoning is this: 'Something is not an aspect of an activity unless it serves to individuate that activity' (ibid.: 100). As most sports appear to lack aesthetic features, Ziff thinks, the aesthetic is not an aspect of sport (ibid.: 94). If we do approach sport with an aesthetic attitude, however, we hazard 'fundamentally distort[ing] the experience of sport' (Edgar 2015: 72) by thereby attending to the formal beauty of athletic movements without regard for the competitive context that makes them athletic in the first place. The concern here is that if we try to do sport aesthetics at all, we will necessarily fail to address sport *as* sport.

What should be made of such a rejection of sport aesthetics? First, it could be that even if most instances of sport are aesthetically neutral or uninteresting, this does not imply that they are not governed by aesthetic norms. As I argue in Chapter 5, for instance, principles of game design are informed by aesthetic considerations, which dovetails with what Mumford calls 'the aesthetic hypothesis: that *aesthetic considerations are essential to the being of sport and continue to shape its development*' (2014: 183, original emphasis). The suggestion is that all instances of sport *may* have aesthetic aspects despite the commonality of plainness and ugliness in many athletic events. Second, we may note along with Mumford (2012: 19) that Ziff's is a 'dubious principle that only something that individuated an activity could be an aspect of it', as it would imply that 'nutrition was not an aspect of eating and reproduction not an aspect of sex' (ibid.: 20, citing Cooper 1978: 52). Likewise, an aesthetic appreciation of sport, including its dramatic qualities, need not ignore and may in fact *depend* on keeping the competitive nature of sport firmly in mind. To these considerations I can add a further reductio of Ziff's view. Because not all artworks or landscapes are aesthetically appreciable either, Ziff's principle implies that the aesthetic is an aspect *neither* of art *nor* of nature and that it would be misguided to do research into the aesthetics of art or nature or to seek in art or nature those special experiences in which we commune with beauty. Against such skepticism, then, I conclude that sport aesthetics, including this volume, remains a playable and potentially rewarding field for sporting philosophers.

Note

1 See for example Welsch (1999: 213): sport 'obviously represents a striking example of today's aestheticization of the everyday', although this sits uncomfortably with a later claim: 'Sport is as distant from ordinary life as is art' (ibid.: 223). The latter claim echoes Kreft's view (2012: 228), which itself echoes Huizinga on play, that sport is separate from everyday life. The right middle ground is that sport is closer to everyday life than rarified artgoing experiences but more special and engaging than the truly mundane parts of existence.

References

Cooper, W. (1978) 'Do Sports Have an Aesthetic Aspect?', *Journal of the Philosophy of Sport*, 5: 51–5.

Edgar, A. (2015) 'Aesthetics of Sport', in M. McNamee and W. J. Morgan (eds.) *Routledge Handbook of the Philosophy of Sport*, New York: Routledge, pp. 69–80.

Kreft, L. (2012) 'Sport as Drama', *Journal of the Philosophy of Sport*, 39 (2): 219–34.

Mumford, S. (2012) *Watching Sport: Aesthetics, Ethics and Emotion*, New York: Routledge.

Mumford, S. (2014) 'The Aesthetics of Sport', in C. R. Torres (ed.) *The Bloomsbury Companion to the Philosophy of Sport*, London: Bloomsbury, pp. 180–94.

Welsch, W. (1999) 'Sport – Viewed Aesthetically, and Even as Art?', *Filozofski Vestnik*, *20* (2): 213–36.

Ziff, P. (1974) 'A Fine Forehand', *Journal of the Philosophy of Sport*, *1*: 92–109.

1 Five-level analysis

Aesthetic appreciation involves taking a type of pleasure in experiencing something one judges to be beautiful or artistic. Notice that 'beauty' and 'art' are not coextensive terms. Just as beauty fails to imply art (not everything beautiful is a work of art), so too art fails to imply beauty (not every artwork is beautiful). In the philosophical tradition, aesthetic pleasure is distinguished from ordinary pleasure. Where the latter is self-interested, the former is disinterested; for example, our pleasure in a painting is aesthetic to the extent that we appreciate its formal (e.g., line and color) or representational (e.g., subject and symbol) properties, but not to the extent that we value it as an investment or a means to make our friends jealous. Taking a kind of pleasure in beauty for its own sake rather than in realizing some instrumental purpose is, at least on a traditional account, what makes for aesthetic rather than some other form of appreciation.[1] On a pragmatist account, however, we might see aesthetic experience not as something that is separate from everyday life and concerns but as continuous with these purposes, a difference of degree rather than kind. We may see the aesthetic, in other words, as a more unified and intense form of otherwise mundane experience (Dewey 1980: 36–7, 43).

Whatever our particular theoretical orientation toward understanding the nature of our aesthetic experiences, we as human beings can take such pleasure in a wide variety of objects, often expectedly, often idiosyncratically. One thing we often take such delight in is movement. Note how the beauty of motion is so memorably rendered in Stanley Kubrick's *2001: A Space Odyssey*, particularly as brought out by Strauss's 'The Blue Danube' waltz. Closer to home, in contrast to the motion of inanimate natural objects and artifacts, is the movement of nonhuman creatures: the hovering hummingbird, the galloping horse, the high-diving osprey. We also can take aesthetic pleasure in the movements, particularly in the *skilled* movements, of human beings, whether a dancer's routine appreciated for its own sake or the precise movement of an athlete achieving a prescribed objective.

It is the last, the aesthetic dimensions of human movement, that is the central focus here, particularly in the realm of sport. To begin with, observe that there are various levels of analysis at which it makes sense to speak of the aesthetic appreciation of movements. I propose, in fact, a five-level analysis (5-LA) for sport aesthetics.[2] These levels are distinguishable but overlapping, so that properties at any one level may be irrelevant to but otherwise may affect the properties at other levels. For example, the elegance of an athlete's movements may be appreciable both in itself and in conjunction with an appreciation of their physique. So too, if opposing sides face off in competition, the aesthetic qualities of their movements can enhance the dramatic power of the contest – and vice versa. These differences should also be conceived of as stratified *levels* instead of, say, mere factors because they constitute successive abstractions from the body through what it does to the meaning of such performances.

Let us turn to the levels themselves.

Level 1: physique

At the first, most concrete level, then, is the athlete's body, affected by practice and conditioning needed to excel in a certain kind of performance but whose form and other observable attributes may be appreciated apart from any actual skilled performance, as well as informing appreciation of such skilled performance. This is not new and dates back in the Western tradition to classical antiquity two and a half millennia ago. Think Greek sculpture.[3] In the first place, we are right to think of the athlete's physique rather than the body more generally: a lean, muscular, flexible, skilled, capable physique. Other features, such as those of the face, may in a sport context take on a secondary importance in an overall assessment of physical appearance. Beautiful masses, forms, proportions, and symmetries may be appreciated in physique and face alike, which may factor into scoring in aesthetic sports like figure skating and gymnastics. Properties like bilateral symmetry and proportions such as the golden ratio (about 1.62 to 1) are things we are hardwired to appreciate in bodies and faces, and when we assess physical pulchritude, these tend to inform our responses subconsciously.

The form of an athlete's body suggests its function, not only because of biological design but partly also, and more so, because it is through practice that the unconditioned body has been changed into one more capable of its intended physical tasks. We can appreciate such physicality in athletic photography as well as sculpture, with the athlete in repose or in frozen abstraction in the process of executing skills. Such a corporeal focus is intensified in sports where the required attire reveals or stresses in outline precisely those physical characteristics that are necessary for and reinforced by exceptional performance. Some sports indeed even require at elite and lesser competitive levels physiques that have the right look for the sport in question. Unlike the various body types that can be found in, say, baseball or golf, aesthetic sports like diving and endurance sports like marathon running tend to approach the virtual homogeneity of a single specific body profile. Only certain bodies will measure up, either as a matter of performance or as a matter of appearance (and this raises some difficult epistemological and ethical questions, some of which will be broached later). Hence you find biases against unathletic-looking physiques and in favor of those that are *hyper*athletic-looking, in truth irrespective of actual performance, even in sports like baseball and golf where such appearances are irrelevant or even detrimental to performance. Thus, aesthetic preferences may reveal biases subject to correction by transpersonal standards of not only rational but aesthetic judgment.

We can appreciate how physiques are likewise abstractable from yet informative of sport aesthetics by considering bodybuilding, which I consider to be a pseudosport, although there is no doubt that weight*lifting* competitions (e.g., Olympic, power), rather than posing a body built by weightlifting, count as sports. Where sports are competitions of physical skill, bodybuilding competitions, however much gym sweat and cutting strategy goes into preparation, are pageants whose outcome is determined by look alone, not skill as well. Nonetheless, the common enough desire to count bodybuilding as a legitimate sport is based on the undeniable athletic *look* of its competitors, irrespective of their natural sport skills or actual weightlifting capacities. We might consider the bodybuilt physique – sometimes body 'sculpture' – along quasi-architectural lines, where natural design has been modified within natural constraints (even if artificially enhanced) according to the builder's intention, a vision of the ideal form. The poses of those competing in bodybuilding certainly *suggest* athletic prowess, just like the preparatory and finishing poses of true athletes, and so share in the silences, if not the sounds, of the music of athletics.

Level 2: movement

Although it is the body that grounds sport aesthetics and allows it at the same time to take flight in what athletes *do*, it is this second level of analysis, that of movement, that we think of – with some justification – as the basic object of beauty in sport. Here the motion of objects, such as the elegant curve of a well-struck soccer ball into the goal, become meaningful as resulting from, as part of, an athlete's or team's actions. Unlike mere motions of the body, movement is done with agency, in other words intentionally, by its subject. The resulting curve of the struck ball is but a part of the player's strike, and this movement and intended result, when successful, constitute the action of the beautiful goal.[4]

At the level of sporting movement it is less the actions themselves than how those actions are performed that admits of aesthetic qualification. In many cases in sport a movement, even an otherwise successful one, may be graceful or awkward, fluid or robotic, inspired or lackluster. In the philosophy of art, such aesthetic properties are usually understood as *supervening* on natural, nonaesthetic properties. What this means is that an aesthetic property, say grace, cannot change without there being a corresponding change in a lower-level property, say precision. If two figure skaters perform the same program or movement, a triple axel for instance, one gracefully and the other awkwardly, that will be because, for instance, the movement of one is less precise (or what have you) than the other's. Even if it is often difficult to specify in a particular instance what the relevant lower-level properties are, their presence or absence may still be cited in accounting for our aesthetic judgment. ('She stumbled on the landing, making her jump awkward'.) It would be remiss here not to mention the highly contextual nature of aesthetic properties in sport. The same crossover turn may count as graceful in ice hockey but not ice dance, the same sidestep graceful in the boxing ring but not on the gymnastics floor.

However, it is not just aesthetic properties like grace that are aesthetically appreciable. It is also possible to appreciate from an aesthetic point of view the natural nonaesthetic properties on which aesthetic properties supervene, properties such as speed, balance, and power, and these may not be aesthetically appealing in some cases though they may be in others. Joe Frazier might have lacked the grace of a Muhammad Ali, but the impressive power of his own style still strikes many in the boxing world as beautiful, even if it is not the beauty of grace. It may be considered beautiful *that* Smokin' Joe could generate such power even if such style is inconsistent with the aesthetic appeal of other pugilists. Although indeed anything can be considered from an aesthetic point of view, only some things may reasonably count as aesthetically piquant from that point of view. A clumsy, weak boxing movement would be unlikely to prompt aesthetic pleasure.

The potential beauty of athletic movement is stressed by different kinds of technological abstraction and experiential enhancement. Consider, for instance, the use of strobe photography to show the successive stages of skilled movement, as though we were seeing it timelessly, as a four-dimensional whole extended through spacetime. Consider also the use of slow-motion video playback and the highlight reel technique of repeating choice clips, both of which give viewers the chance to savor at leisure the unfolding intricacies of attention-worthy individual efforts and team plays. Such enhancements allow the average fan to approximate what expert eyes are more likely to appreciate in real time, though even expert judgment can benefit from video assistance, as is evinced by the increasing use of video assistance in refereeing and judging.

Level 3: performance

It is crucial to distinguish, in most cases at least, particular sport movements, attempts, and plays from the more abstract level of performance. First, most sport performances include a variety of different movements. Second, and relatedly, a winning or beautiful athletic display can include individual efforts that are unsuccessful or unbeautiful. Performance *comprises* movements. The aesthetic appeal of a sport performance considered broadly may emerge as a gestalt despite local kinetic imperfections, and even when there is no particular constitutive movement that qualifies as beautiful. The same is true of works of art. A painting or film, for example, may earn critical acclaim despite identifiable flaws in the brushwork or acting or despite a total lack of individual elements that merit such approval. The beauty of a sport performance or an artwork can reside in how it all comes together, in how it just jells. Supposing otherwise is the fallacy of division, just as inferring overall quality from local beauty is the fallacy of composition.

Performance itself can be appreciated in single instances or across multiple events, with both types potentially speaking to considerations of *style*. Performance style may be appreciated in an individual athlete in an overall sense (e.g., Ali's graceful boxing) or in more specific marks of distinction (e.g., Abdul-Jabbar's patented skyhook). In both cases, uniqueness of style seems stamped by the athlete's personality.[5] An athletic style may also extend beyond individuals and characterize group strategies and styles of play (e.g., Brazilian soccer). Athletes in competitive ball sports are sometimes praised for their adaptive creativity in responding to the chaotic order of game dynamics, and here awkward-looking quirky styles and techniques (e.g., reliever Kent Tekulve's underarm delivery) are tolerated, even praised as strategically sound, since opponents are less accustomed to them. Oddly, the same does not hold in sport subcultures like golf, where distinctive techniques departing from the presumed ideal form tend to be denigrated *despite* their efficacy and what is for most the unfeasibility of the classic swing.[6] In aesthetic sports, however, for scoring purposes it is sensible that ideal forms are prescribed and expected to be embodied or approximated by athletes who, for this reason, perhaps paradoxically, may often find it harder to realize a distinctive style.

Just as we saw at the level of movement, where nonaesthetic properties may be aesthetically appreciable, so too at this level can we find the sheer achievement of an athlete's performance to be beautiful. With especially rare or extremely difficult performances, for instance, a championship win, a record-setting run, a perfect ten, and so on, the performance may take on a kind of aura associated with its difficulty and rarity. If we find ourselves moved by the fact that human beings – or some of us, anyway – are capable of such feats, our aesthetic appreciation at this level may be appropriately informed by higher levels. In many sports it will be hard to see the beauty of what athletes are doing independent of understanding the rules that constrain their behavior, although – to use Kant's terminology somewhat elastically – aesthetic sport performances have a kind of free beauty irrespective of function, whereas purposive sports have a dependent beauty that requires but does not reduce to instrumental efficacy (2005: 48–9). A dive can prompt aesthetic response even if one doesn't know the rules of diving, and the most beautiful program might not win a figure skating competition. But if one doesn't know the rules, it is hard to see the draw of hard defensive tackles or brutal punches, and the most beautiful deke cannot fail to leave the defender undone. It would also be hard to feel full awe at a record-setting performance without considering its significance *as* unprecedented. Just as an athlete's physique and specific movements may inform our aesthetic appreciation of their performance – in a single contest, over a season, or an entire career – so too it may also be informed by our appreciation of the framework in which those performances occur or the corresponding and further significance attached to them, as we will see.

Level 4: framework

Even more abstract, at the fourth level we may appreciate aesthetically the *framework* in which sport performances occur and without which such behavior would appear as rather nonsensical. After all, from a certain distance most cultural practices seem pointless or utterly silly. 'Context' here is too nebulous a term to be especially useful, not only because it includes certain elements from the next level up (Level 5) as well but because the envisioned framework is more nuanced in being partly physical, partly formal, partly institutional: differences glossed over by the broad term 'context' on its own.

To begin with the physical, I have in mind the setting where sport performances happen, not the types of places but the specific actual locales and not only the playing surface itself but the surrounding area as well. In outdoor venues weather is also a factor. Consider the following pregame description from the celebrated sportswriter Roger Angell: 'the sunlit field before us is a thick, springy green – an old diamond, beautifully kept up. The grass continues beyond the low chain-link fence . . . extending itself on the right-field side into a rougher, featureless sward that terminates in a low line of distant trees. . . . We are almost in the country' (2010: 3). Plausibly the most important part of an athletic setting that can prompt aesthetic response all by itself is venue architecture, whether the sloping links of a well-designed golf course or various symmetries and peculiarities of stadium design. The sports fan's specific vantage point also matters, of course, as does one's place among the crowd, if there is one, and if one is actually attending a live event in person. Relevant aspects of the physical setting also include athletic attire, equipment, apparatus, and the playing area itself, though, since the rules affect these to a certain degree, we are abutting on what I call the formal part of the framework of sport.

The formal framework of sport should be construed largely in terms of the rules, as they structure game activity, and in terms of clustered types of sports that share structural similarities. Examples of clustered types include aesthetic sports in contrast to purposive sports and between what Kretchmar calls E games, which are delimited by events (e.g., innings, holes) and T games, which are delimited by time (e.g., quarters, periods).[7] If we understand sports as differentiated, if not defined, by their rules as structuring consequently distinct activities, it becomes evident how partly aesthetic judgments about such structures inform individual sport preferences. First, those who invent or modify games – gamewrights – are guided in their design choices by an aesthetic sense of what rules would yield quality games. As Elliott maintains, 'those who determine what the rules of a game are to be have a responsibility to safeguard the possibility of the emergence of beauty' (1974: 113–4). Likewise, the rules of a fan's preferred sports structure those activities he finds pleasing to watch. That soccer is the world's most popular sport is partly explained by its aesthetic value as the beautiful game.[8] (I have a hypothesis about why it is the world's most popular sport, but this will have to wait till Chapter 4.)

Of course, the dominant view in philosophy of sport is that what structures sport activity is not exactly the rules themselves or social conventions but the *logic* of the game, how the rules are best interpreted and applied.[9] This suggests another structural facet at the framework level, consisting in various sport institutions whose influence on various sport practices is evident and whose aesthetic dimension is also appreciable. If we consider sport history, for example, we can see how the place of an athletic performance in that history may be aesthetically informative. A performance may be considered more beautiful when it succeeds at setting a record or has some other mark of distinction in the history of the sport. Think of how a performance gains in appeal just because it takes place at the Olympics or of how the torch ceremony at the games reinforces via spectacular pageantry both their historical gravitas and their aesthetic richness.

Level 5: significance

At the fifth level of analysis, beyond the framework that makes sense of sport movements and performances, we find the significance discovered in and attributed to them. Sport's institutional framework already provides it with a kind of internal significance and so overlaps with this fifth level, which is characterized rather in terms external significance that, despite being rooted in sport, nonetheless breaks through sport's interior confines to occupy a place of greater import, including psychological significance, broad moral significance, and cultural significance.

There are two kinds of psychological significance (at least) that should be distinguished here. When a sporting event holds our attention in a kind of breathless wonder, it has a dramatic significance that less engaging events fail to match. Such dramatic significance is psychological in that it depends upon the inner tension of uncertainty of a game's outcome and on the observer being invested in some way in witnessing that outcome. Whether such tension, which is released finally at the denouement, counts in a strict sense as true drama, and even perhaps as tragedy, is up for debate (e.g., Culbertson 2017). We can distinguish the transpersonal quality of the drama of sport from the more individual quality of a fan's personal significance. Part of what makes ice hockey aesthetically appealing to me draws on my own unique experience, having played it in my youth, watched it live and on television, and amassed a particular collection of hockey cards. Others may have had similar experiences, played the game at higher levels, or gathered superior card collections, but mine nonetheless retain a special significance. Such personal and dramatic significance comes together in the figure of the partisan, who roots for a particular team or athlete rather than holding a purist attitude and taking enjoyment in no matter whose athletic excellence (Mumford 2012: 9–10).

The aesthetic power of sport can also be affected by its moral significance, specifically a function of the moral status of its players as expressed in their participation. Although we tend to think of aesthetic and ethical values as entirely distinct, in certain domains like sport there seems to be a tighter connection between the two types of value (ibid.: 68). Positive moral traits tend to enhance the aesthetic appeal of a sport performance, if it demonstrates courage, a work ethic, or sportsmanship, say.[10] On the other hand, negative moral characteristics, such as wanton brutality or cheating, tend to diminish our aesthetic appreciation, to the point of finding *ugly* performances that would otherwise be beautiful. We should be wary, though, of letting either aesthetic or moral judgment hastily or unfairly influence the other.

Sometimes moral significance is limited to the appreciation of an individual performance or athlete, though sometimes it takes on a wider significance. When it does, a moral significance can acquire a representative or symbolic function and become culturally significant as well. Part of the aesthetic appeal of Jesse Owens's amazing performances at the 1936 Olympics lies in the cultural context, taking place in Berlin during the Third Reich, under the auspices of the Nazis, and overseen by Hitler himself. Without such deplorable circumstances, Owens's performances would have lacked some of their profundity and poignancy. On the negative side, in our culture women's sports tend to be regarded unfairly as both less important *and* less appealing to watch (although figure skating is a notable exception, women's events being more popular than men's, for reasons that are less than edifying). Hence our aesthetic responses to sport may be enhanced by appropriately progressive attitudes and practices and retarded by unjustly conservative ones.

Payoff and objections

Putting all these levels together, we can visualize in outline the five-level analysis (or 5-LA) that I propose (see Table 1.1). Again, these are levels of abstraction from the body and should not be construed otherwise as a hierarchy in which higher levels necessarily trump lower ones. Though

Table 1.1 Five-level analysis

Level		
5 Significance	(e.g., drama)
4 Framework	(e.g., rules)
3 Performance	(e.g., style)
2 Movement	(e.g., grace)
1 Physique	(e.g., form)

I trust this analysis strikes the reader as having some conceptual fidelity or intuitive plausibility, yet that is only part of its justification. Part of its justification lies too in its theoretical payoff, which will require most of the rest of the book to explore in enough detail.

Still, though, before addressing a few likely objections to 5-LA, it is worth remarking on two points in connection with its theoretical plausibility and payoff. First, notice that 5-LA is not unique to sport but may also be applied to other domains where human movement appeals to our aesthetic sensibilities, domains such as dance. We can appreciate for instance the lean form of a dancer's physique, the vitality of her movements, the athleticism of a style like Baryshnikov's, the venue architecture or dance tradition that frames performances, or the dramatic and symbolic significance of the embodied choreography. Applicability to cognate domains suggests avoiding the pitfall of a merely idiosyncratic or ad hoc plausibility.

Second, much of 5-LA's theoretical payoff is likely to come from locating heterogeneous theories and debates on the same conceptual map, thereby giving fresh perspective and purchase on them. As we will explore in subsequent chapters, for instance, theoretical debates about grace may come down to the type of framework (Level 4) in question; likewise, we may see the purist and partisan not as expressing different attitudes toward the worthiness of being an aesthete but as embracing – rightly or wrongly – different aesthetic levels (Level 3 and Level 5, respectively) and indeed different theories of aesthetic experience. Though these remarks are admittedly brief and promissory, they offer a glimpse of some of the book's forthcoming payoff.

Before leaving this chapter behind, I will now raise and briefly respond to three possible objections. First is what I will call the deflationary objection, the idea that 5-LA simply violates Occam's Razor in needlessly multiplying levels of analysis. Why not, the objector might think, collapse 5-LA into just *two* levels, movement and context? By doing so, the objection runs, we acknowledge the context sensitivity of aesthetic properties like grace and can seemingly account for why the same movement – such as a crossover – could count as graceful in hockey but not in figure skating: different context, different aesthetic. What the objector is missing here, however, is that this move of collapsing four levels into context alone does not help to explain the data but merely rephrases them, in effect passing the buck. If anything, 5-LA does not go *far* enough, for we could easily take each subtype at the framework and significance levels (Level 4 and Level 5) as separate strata in their own right. Limiting the analysis to five levels was not a necessary but a pragmatic choice, and I take this to be a mark in its favor rather than a detriment.

Second is what I call the normative objection, that 5-LA is normatively silent or false. In other words, it may help us characterize differences in aesthetic preference, but it seems to tell us nothing about aesthetic standards, about which preferences we *ought* to have. On 5-LA, we may see a quirky technique as ugly (Level 2) or original (Level 3), but it appears useless in helping us decide which interpretation is better. In response, though, part of the theoretical task is arguably to account for such preferences. Plus, we may decide between discrepant aesthetic responses if it turns out, for instance on some third level, that one of the two represents bias. In purposive sport frameworks (Level 4), it may prove fitting to champion diversity and value unusual but effective techniques as original rather than ugly. Hence 5-LA is neither descriptivism nor subjectivism but rather a nuanced pluralism.

Last is what I call the etymological objection, according to which aesthetics is only about appearance (Levels 1–2), not about interpretation (Levels 3–5); since the ancient Greek word '*aisthēsis*' means sensation, not understanding, aesthetics properly understood is really about uninterpreted pleasant sensations. 'A rose by any other name . . .', as the objector might misquote. Here athletic physiques and movements remain proper objects of aesthetic appreciation, but only considered in isolation from such categorizations as *athlete*. Of course, to deny current usage because it departs from earlier usage is to commit the genetic fallacy. That said, we should of course acknowledge the Aristotelean tradition in which what we now call aesthetics is not just about appearances but also about our emotional and cognitive responses to them. If we consider pointed examples like 1987's Gretzky-to-Lemieux Canada Cup–winning goal, it is hopeless to try reducing the aesthetic power of such a scene to mere bodily movements having nothing to do with the event's closing-minute dramatic timing, international profile, or renown of the players – a good play, yes, but a sublime moment. Significance shapes beauty. Besides smelling sweet, roses are also symbols of romantic love, of secrecy ('*sub rosa*'), of royal houses, and so on. A rose by any other name would smell as sweet, but a rose as any other symbol would not.

Notes

1 Aesthetic disinterest is canonically articulated by Kant (2005: 34–5).
2 Some material in this chapter, including this proposal in somewhat inchoate form, first appeared in Burrow and Holt (2017). Compare with Mumford's threefold distinction among levels of 'aesthetic abstraction': (1) motion, form, and grace; (2) higher-level, abstract forms; and (3) drama, to which he adds a separate category of innovation and genius (2014: 187–90).
3 For discussion of appreciating the sculptural qualities of athletic bodies as an inheritance from classical antiquity, see Gumbrecht (2006: 153–7) and Lowe (1977: 4–7, 10–17).
4 This is not to say that *all* aspects of deliberate actions are intended or foreseen, as that would be impossible.
5 For more on the aesthetic appeal of individual athletes' styles, see Boxill (1984).
6 See Holt and Holt (2010: 217). More on this in Chapter 6.
7 This position was first articulated in Kretchmar (2005).
8 Witness an entire recent special issue of *Sport, Ethics and Philosophy* devoted to the aesthetics of soccer: S. Borge et al. (2015).
9 For Simon's classic account of this position, see Simon et al. (2014: 31–4).
10 Usage in the philosophy of sport still prefers 'sportsmanship' over gender-neutral terms, partly because 'sportspersonship' is utterly inelegant. My suggestion is the neologism 'sportitude' (i.e., 'sporting' + 'attitude', with connotations of 'fortitude').

References

Angell, R. (2010) 'The Web of the Game', in D. Remnick (ed.) *The Only Game in Town: Sportswriting from the New Yorker*, New York: Modern Library, pp. 3–22.

Borge, S., Smith, M. and Vaage, M. B. (eds.) (2015) *Sport, Ethics and Philosophy* (Special Issue on the Aesthetics of Football), *9* (2): 93–232.

Boxill, J. M. (1984) 'Beauty, Sport, and Gender', *Journal of the Philosophy of Sport, 11* (1): 36–47.

Burrow, S. and Holt, J. (2017) 'Aesthetic Dimensions of Virtue in Sport and Martial Arts', Paper presented at the International Association for the Philosophy of Sport, Whistler, Canada.

Culbertson, L. (2017) 'Purism and the Category of "the Aesthetic": The Drama Argument', *Journal of the Philosophy of Sport, 44* (1): 1–14.

Dewey, J. (1980) *Art as Experience*, New York: Perigee.

Elliott, R. K. (1974) 'Aesthetics and Sport', in H. T. A. Whiting and D. W. Masterson (eds.) *Readings in the Aesthetics of Sport*, London: Lepus, pp. 107–16.

Gumbrecht, H. U. (2006) *In Praise of Athletic Beauty*, Cambridge, MA: Harvard University Press.

Holt, J. and Holt, L. E. (2010) 'The "Ideal" Swing, the "Ideal" Body: Myths of Optimization', in A. Wible (ed.) *Golf and Philosophy: Lessons from the Links*, Lexington: University Press of Kentucky, pp. 209–20.

Kant, I. (2005) *Critique of Judgment*, J. H. Bernard (trans.), New York: Dover.

Kretchmar, R. S. (2005) 'Game Flaws', *Journal of the Philosophy of Sport*, *32* (1): 36–48.

Lowe, B. (1977) *The Beauty of Sport: A Cross-Disciplinary Inquiry*, Englewood Cliffs: Prentice-Hall.

Mumford, S. (2012) *Watching Sport: Aesthetics, Ethics and Emotion*, New York: Routledge.

Mumford, S. (2014) 'The Aesthetics of Sport', in C. R. Torres (ed.) *The Bloomsbury Companion to the Philosophy of Sport*, London: Bloomsbury, pp. 180–94.

Simon, R. L., Torres, C. R. and Hager, P. F. (2014) *Fair Play: The Ethics of Sport* (4th Ed.), New York: Westview.

2 Grace notes

In the poem 'Ode to Sport', written for the Stockholm 1912 Olympics, authors Georges Hohrod and M. Eschbach (Pierre de Coubertin) extol sport for its many positive attributes, for the values it fosters. The first stanza describes the birth of sport in the murky distant past, followed by each successive stanza that takes as its subject one of sport's ascribed values: justice, audacity, honor, joy, fecundity, progress, and peace. Before all of these, however, at the top of the list is aesthetic value. Sport is extolled as Beauty, as the architect of the human body made sublime by physical activity, as the master of balance and proportion, as creating harmony, as uniting movement and rhythm, strength and grace, suppleness and power (2000: 29). If there is any remaining doubt that aesthetics lies at the very heart of our love of sport, let it be put to rest. To seriously address aesthetic properties in sport, however, will require first taking a theoretical step back.

Aesthetic value contrasts with other sorts of value, and values generally are distinguished from facts, the way things are. The latter is the principled fact/value distinction, facts being states of affairs as they are (e.g., This *is* a martini), values concerning rather the way things ought to be (This is a *good* martini). I may have another martini when dining out, but although this may give me pleasure, that doesn't mean I ought to have another. There may be moral reasons against my having another martini, say if I plan to drive home. There may be prudential reasons too. Maybe I am dining with colleagues and another martini would go against my better judgment. There may be aesthetic reasons too. I might find unappealing the imagined scenario of being less in control of my faculties. In general, we distinguish matters of fact from matters of value, and among values we distinguish among moral goodness, rational intelligence, and aesthetic beauty.

The relationship between matters of value and matters of fact is an issue of philosophical debate generally and specifically in terms of the relationship between aesthetic and nonaesthetic properties. Following Sibley, aesthetic properties include '*unified, balanced, integrated, lifeless, serene, somber, dynamic, powerful, vivid, delicate, moving, trite, sentimental, tragic*' (1959: 421, original emphasis). We might notice the partial overlap with the properties mentioned in 'Ode to Sport' (balance and power), though more important is the complementarity of the two lists. Even though, on Sibley's account, nonaesthetic properties will not guarantee the presence of aesthetic properties, some natural properties will count toward and others against aesthetic ascription.[1] For instance, if a piece of music is in a minor key, that will count toward it being sad, but if it is in a major key, that can count against such ascription. Perhaps some aesthetic properties are reducible to, or at least dependent on, certain nonaesthetic properties, and in this light I turn to a particular focused debate in sport aesthetics.

The grace debate

One of the properties of movement we value in sport and other arenas is grace. Some movements and styles are graceful, others effective but graceless, other still ineffective, even clumsy. Grace in movement, then, suggests skill, control, apparent effortlessness, and yet also at the same time a kind of spontaneity, playfulness, and freedom. For a number of decades now in the philosophy of sport, there has been a slowly evolving debate about the nature of graceful movement, and in this section I will trace the major positions in this debate so as to situate subsequent commentary and thereby motivate a proposal to help resolve it.[2]

As does arguably sport aesthetics itself, the grace debate begins with the seminal work of David Best.[3] Sport aesthetics over the past four decades or so has been conducted largely in terms framed by Best. It is to Best for example that we owe our current conception and terminology of the distinction between aesthetic sports, in which aesthetic judgment figures into determining the outcomes, and purposive sports, in which such judgment does not so figure. Best takes aesthetic sports to provide the basis for theoretical elaboration: 'In figure skating, diving, synchronized swimming, trampolining, and Olympic gymnastics, it is of the first importance that there should be no wasted effort and no superfluous motion' (1978: 106). In purposive sports, aesthetic appeal is not necessary yet remains both appreciable and desirable despite comparative marginalization.

In hockey, for instance, two garbage goals always beat one beautiful goal, although we still enjoy beautiful goals. A champion runner likewise may have a jerky, ungainly style, in which case the apparently superfluous parts of her gait will strike observers as aesthetic flaws (Best's example is the runner Zátopek). As far as economy and efficiency of movement are concerned, however, for Best, 'the same consideration applies to our aesthetic appreciation of sports of the purposive kind' (ibid.) and thus advocates what Mumford calls a functionality account of grace – indeed of aesthetic appeal generally – in sport. On Best's account, aesthetic appeal in sport is a function of 'economy and efficiency of effort' or the 'graceful economy' of movement (ibid.: 107). Though this wasn't Best's concern, we may speculate whether his theory can be extended to movements apart from the domain of sport.

In fact, perhaps Best's most strident critic on this matter, Christopher Cordner, begins his critique by noting examples outside the domain of sport. We might consider a gamboling fawn to be graceful, for instance, even though there is no identifiable purpose at which the fawn aims; it makes no sense to speak here of economy and efficiency of movement, as there is no identifiable end the achievement of which could help us ascertain functionality, yet the fawn's grace itself is readily appreciable (1984: 304).[4] Cordner also raises the hypothetical case of a bowling machine that is designed to move with perfect economy and precision but that would naturally be ungraceful (ibid.: 305). Cordner's key counterexample to Best's account is the tennis star Martina Navratilova, the dominant player of her time in women's tennis, whose performance style Cordner describes as lacking grace despite its power and efficiency (ibid.). Presumably his verdict on the current great Serena Williams would be similar, for, despite her dominance, hers is not a particularly graceful style even if her performances are otherwise aesthetically appealing. By contrast, an elite player from Navratilova's era who played gracefully, at least in Cordner's estimation, is John McEnroe (ibid.: 310). (One current and rather more plausible example is Roger Federer.) Notwithstanding McEnroe's notorious penchant for unsporting conduct on the court, his playing style is graceful, in Cordner's view, not because of its efficacy but rather because it demonstrates 'unity of being in the performance' and 'harmony or accord in all its elements. In a graceful display, everything comes together in a harmonious whole' (ibid.: 308). Cordner therefore intends to supplant Best's account with one that stresses the smooth integration of different segments of movement instead of its economy or efficiency.

Another position proposed by Davis is motivated by his focused criticism of Cordner's view, though the complaint applies no less to Best's or any other attempt to theoretically ground or desuperficialize athletic grace. For Davis, Cordner's view leaves open the possibility, which it ought not to, that the alleged theoretical basis of grace, in this case unity of being, can be present without grace and vice versa. Indeed, as Davis has it this implies the possibility of 'fool's grace', which seems to be graceful but, like fool's gold, lacks the right underlying essence (2001: 92). In other words, we could be wrong about movements that seem graceful but in reality fail to be so. But Davis takes this notion to be incoherent, as there simply is no such thing as fool's grace. For Davis, any movement will be graceful just in case it appears graceful to us, and we are mistaken to suppose there is anything deeper at work than this. In the realm of pleasing appearances, either in sport or in general, our shared aesthetic response will suffice. If we agree that some movement or style is graceful, whether a Comaneci on the gymnastics floor or an Ali in the boxing ring, we are misguided to seek or even presume a theoretical depth beneath this level of appearance.

The next stage in the development of this debate is offered by Mumford, who agrees with Davis that, as it stands, Cordner's account of grace is inadequate as well as somewhat vague and who concedes to Davis that there is no such thing as fool's grace. Even if aesthetic properties do not exist as metaphysically independent of our response to them, this doesn't imply in matters of taste a pure sort of subjectivism, which Mumford attributes to David Hume, by which properties like grace are nothing more than expressions of subjective response to pleasing appearances. For one thing, 'isn't there some difference between us finding some "pleasing appearances" to be of grace and other pleasing appearances to be of speed and power?' (2012: 27). For another, surely there is reason why we approximate consensus on whether some styles are graceful and why we often offer reasons to explicate or justify our verdicts in the face of aesthetic disagreement (ibid.: 27–8), however stubborn. Mumford's positive account, though not an elaborated theory of grace like Best's or Cordner's, acknowledges the need for the analytic depth eschewed by Davis: 'We could analyse further and find, for instance, that graceful movements should be fluid rather than jerky, or that a graceful pose must exhibit balance, equilibrium, poise, and effortlessness' (ibid.: 29). Putting his position thus, Mumford seems to ally himself with Best, since it is an apparently superfluous, jerky motion in Zátopek's gait that by Best's reckoning renders it graceless.

It is here that the grace debate stands, a succession of four different positions, each later account being motivated partly by apparent flaws in its predecessors: Best's *functional* account as economy and efficiency of movement and effort, Cordner's *integrated* account as harmonious unity of athletic elements, Davis's *surface* account as an unanalyzable simple expressing viewer response, and Mumford's *deep* account as implied by relevant features of aesthetic discourse. In contributing to this debate, I will first provide commentary, assessing the relative merits of these positions, before offering my own proposal.

Comments and proposal

Each of the preceding perspectives contains important insights that ideally should be captured in a robust theory of grace while at the same time avoiding associated pitfalls. Returning to Best, I should emphasize that he is not explicitly or necessarily offering a theory of graceful movement specifically but seems instead to outline what it means for sport performance to be aesthetically appealing in a general sense. That Cordner positions him rather as offering a specific theory of grace, that is, as a foil to his own account, is understandable, as is Mumford's acceptance of this interpretation in tracing the history of the debate. Hence presumably for Best for a sporting style to have not just grace but also or otherwise expressiveness, vitality, or any other aesthetic merit would also require economy and efficiency of movement and effort. Viewed this way, objecting that Best's conditions are insufficient for grace doesn't hold, though the corresponding power of his account is thereby diminished.

Leaving that aside, it seems we must admit that something in Best's account is along the right lines if we consider the concept of having *good form* in sport and, correspondingly, also his emphasis that certain properties count against aesthetic attributions. In gymnastics, for instance, part of what it means to perform a prescribed movement pattern correctly is avoiding extraneous motions or efforts to correct such imperfections (e.g., an extra step, a wavering pose). That is, breaking rather than maintaining form in gymnastics will both consist in and be revealed by kinetic superfluity. I believe Best is also right or onto something important when he accounts for a lack of aesthetic appeal in running techniques to be explained in some cases by what seems to be kinetic superfluity. Jerky, unbalanced styles in many sports including running show a lack of good form, and, though later I will discuss such attitudes as potentially *biased*, the connection is a natural one.

Mumford's complaint about Cordner's account suffering from a kind of vagueness may be applied comparably to Best's theory. Consider what it means for movements or efforts to be economical or efficient. Even if we are clear that we are speaking of what *appears* functional in this way rather than actually *being* functional in this way, vagueness remains. Suppose a hockey player may take either a hard stride and curving glide or take two shorter, more direct strides. In the former case we have a more explosive effort and greater distance but fewer movements, and in the latter we have an extra movement but *ex hypothesi* less distance and effort. All else being equal, which is the more graceful, which the more economical and efficient? The answer is not clear, since economy of motion and efficiency of effort appear to come apart here. Likewise, if grace depends on a kind of functional parsimony, on putting in just enough movement and effort to get the job done, consider the following scenario. Sticking with hockey, would a goal be more graceful the more softly rather than decisively the shot was taken? Would it not be more graceful still to deke the goalie despite the extra movement and effort this might entail? Even so, there is something importantly right about Best's account, and it seems plausible that we could recast in sufficiently precise terms the functional basis of a Bestian, if not Best's own, account of grace.

By the same token, however, it seems also that there is something importantly wrong in Best's account, and this is what Cordner's counterexamples of the gamboling fawn and Martina Navratilova zero in on. Grace and functionality pull apart in some contexts, and in a way this is not surprising given the almost axiomatic intuition that the aesthetic properties of movement in sport must be context sensitive; again, a sudden sidestep may be graceful in the boxing ring but not on the gymnastics floor, a crossover turn on the same rink graceful in hockey but not figure skating. What Cordner gets right is that in tennis, say, what matters for grace is not economy or efficiency of effort but rather a kind of integration of movements, what he somewhat fancifully refers to as a 'unity of being'. Indeed, according to Cordner's theory of grace, movements and style are graceful only to the extent that *people* are (1984: 311–2, 2003: 132). Vagueness aside, the account seems to run together quite deliberately two very different ideas: grace in sport as an observable, fluid integration of movements and grace more generally as an inferable inner state whereby a being's personality is integrated with itself and with its bodily expression. Notice that with Cordner's exemplar of grace, John McEnroe, it is far more plausible to see grace in the first sense, grace of *performative* style – in which personality need not enter the picture – rather than attributing a *personal* grace to his entire being considered holistically. Surely McEnroe's is, if anything, a performative rather than personal grace.

This move takes care of Davis's concern about fool's grace in connection with Cordner's theory, as performative style is more directly observable in an athlete's play rather than having to be inferred, with some uncertainty, from her play and general comportment. Still, in contrast to Davis and Mumford, we may insist that we can make sense of the idea of fool's grace. In diving, for instance, an athlete may flex at the waist on entering the water to minimize the appearance of overrotation. To the extent that this may deceive novice observers in real time, and even judges in some cases, we may interpret this as a sort of fool's grace in that it *fakes* some of the virtues – straight entry, minimal splash – of truly graceful dives. We might, with Mumford, also take issue with the notion that in sport aesthetics we are somehow misguided to attempt to theorize beneath pleasing appearances. However, I believe there is also something truly insightful in this idea – if we tweak it a little. Davis may be right in denying that there is a single reductive basis for grace across all sports and beyond the domain of sport itself. Consider the phrase 'grace under fire', for instance. We might find grace in an athlete rising to the occasion of a high-pressure situation and being able to perform *at all* much less as prescribed by some theory of graceful movement.

With Mumford, we find a mostly appropriate take on the preceding literature as well as remarks pregnant with significance. We should also note imperfections, the first of which is an insensitive reading of David Hume, whom Mumford pictures as a kind of pure subjectivist about aesthetic properties, though he is actually an exponent of a view very much like Mumford's. For Hume, aesthetic properties and values are discernible by those with expert taste, which requires 'Strong sense, united to delicate sentiment, improved by practice, perfected by comparison, and cleared of all prejudice' (2002: 44). Such expertise helps resolve disputes in aesthetic ascription, perceiving precisely those sometimes subtle properties that can elude less refined, less practiced, or less impartial tastes. We may be somewhat disappointed that Mumford's view appears rather promissory, positing but not specifying, at least not doing so systematically, deeper properties to account for grace, but he is correct both to posit such properties and to agree with Best that other properties, like jerkiness, count against graceful movement, where still *others* like balance come to the fore in cases of graceful posing. We may also find it peculiar that power, balance, and like properties are mentioned as aesthetic rather than aesthetically *appreciable* properties, given their literal meaning in sport (unlike their metaphorical application to works of art: a poem's strength is not a weightlifter's strength). But the apparent contextualism suggested here is important and worth exploring further.

Turning now to my proposal, notice that poses, whose requisite aesthetic bases Mumford plausibly identifies, reflect functional precision required for grace and indeed success not across the board but specifically in aesthetic rather than purposive sports. In purposive sports, however, such mere functional precision counts *against* ascriptions of grace, for here it is fluid integration of individual components that makes a movement or style graceful. In other words, it is entirely consistent to suppose that Best is right about grace being functional precision in gymnastics and other aesthetic sports *and* that Cordner is right about grace being fluid integration of movements in tennis and other purposive sports. The mistake is in supposing that one type is transposable to the other. In a nutshell, then, my proposal is that grace is functional precision in aesthetic sports and fluid integration in purposive sports. We may supplement this by also including grace under pressure as a kind of poise irrespective of the sport type. The jerkiness of Zátopek's gait counts against grace not because it lacks efficiency but because it lacks fluidity, as with Navratilova's playing style. Aesthetic sports require functional precision because the grace of proper technique and good form are *built in* to prescribed movement patterns rather than, in purposive sports, the aesthetic arising by some means over and above effective technique. For this reason, it is easier to achieve aesthetic appeal in aesthetic sports but harder to achieve a distinctive style, though in purposive sports this is reversed, distinctiveness proving more common than aesthetic piquancy. Effectively splitting the difference between Best and Cordner in this way, we vindicate not only Davis's view that there is no unified basis for grace across all sports events but also Mumford's argument from aesthetic discourse to the need for theoretical depth. Everybody wins – or rather, no one wins everything, but everyone wins something.

Other properties

Again, it seems curious that philosophers of sport have focused on grace rather than any number of other aesthetic and aesthetically appreciable properties. We might share Edgar's suspicion of the term 'beauty' (2013b: 100) in part because it is nebulously realized by more substantive or at least more specific aesthetic properties: grace is beautiful, but so are elegance, harmony, vitality, expressiveness, and so on, and so too we may sometimes similarly appreciate characteristics that are not inherently aesthetic: strength, endurance, flexibility, and so on.[5] Perhaps there has been focus on grace because it seems an aesthetic virtue plausibly expressed across a wide variety of different sports. Other properties, like expressiveness, seem far more limited in scope in the sport domain. In any event, we can accept the complaint regarding nebulousness of the term 'beauty' without also giving up either on the term or on sport aesthetics generally.[6] Appropriate uses of 'beauty' will presuppose further specifiability in terms of finer-grained concepts like grace, and these again need not yield to some naturalistic reduction.

We should also be wary of generalizing hastily from our discussion of grace, my take on which does not necessarily imply the same approach to other aesthetic properties. Although, as I have argued, grace has different underlying bases in different types of sport frameworks, it could turn out that where grace is not, for instance, expressiveness in sport *is* reducible, say, to all and only those sport performances intended to embody and arouse certain forms of emotion. In other words, some aesthetic properties in sport might have the very sort of univocal realization lacked by grace. The same applies more forcefully to nonaesthetic properties that may be aesthetically appreciable, since these will tend toward more standard definitions. For instance, flexibility can be appreciated aesthetically in a variety of sports, and we may define flexibility as 'the intrinsic property of body tissues that determines the range of motion achievable without injury at a joint or group of joints' (Holt et al. 1996: 172). Part of the reason we cannot count such properties as aesthetic is that the properties are present in uninspiring standard cases (e.g., *my* flexibility), not just impressive cases (e.g., a gymnast's flexibility). The power mentioned as 'aesthetic' by both Coubertin and Mumford thus should be construed in either the figurative sense, which is no less apropos of some artworks, or the literal sense only as framed by aesthetic contingency.

Considering aesthetically relevant properties can help make sense of different aesthetic preferences and perhaps also resolve aesthetic disputes. Consider the different major swimming strokes: butterfly, backstroke, breaststroke, and front crawl. I am rather surprised that Best finds the butterfly to be aesthetically *un*appealing in contrast with the more familiar front crawl (1978: 109). In my view this gets things precisely backwards. The most beautiful stroke is the butterfly, not the crawl. I hypothesize that Best prefers the crawl stroke for some of the following reasons: it better resembles bipedal land motion, minimizes inertial lag, and is faster (more 'functional'). The butterfly, however, has many aesthetic virtues, particularly if we consider the technique of a Mary T. Meagher or a Michael Phelps. It is symmetrical, like breaststroke, both with its unique dolphin kick, unlike the crawl's flutter or the breast's frog kick, and in its wing-like arm motion. It is also much harder for most swimmers to do at all, much rarer to see done well (and thus has an 'aura' about it), and requires what internally feels like counterintuitive timing. It is the most explosive of the strokes and most closely resembles animal motion in water and in air. I appeal last to the very terms 'butterfly' and 'front crawl', labels that are not only descriptively accurate but consequently aesthetically revealing. Although for these reasons I affirm that butterfly is the most beautiful stroke in swimming, whether my reasoning constitutes a strong argument against Best or merely elaborates a contrary aesthetic preference, I leave to the reader's judgment.

Another property that is often if not necessarily aesthetically appealing in sport is having a distinctive style. Some distinctive styles present as quirky or even ugly, however successful in purposive terms such techniques may be. For now, I defer discussion of such cases until later in the context of aesthetic bias. We tend to delight in both the signature moves and the general style of outstanding players. Consider Denis Savard's spinorama versus Wayne Gretzky's more general distinctiveness. We may appreciate styles that strike us as playful, whether the comportment of a Usain Bolt or the group style of Brazilian soccer. One badge of distinction is creativity, whether an athlete improvises an inspired play in a game situation or develops a revolutionary technique like Dick Fosbury's flop. This technique, for decades now the standard high-jump technique, is considered a beautiful created form of movement, even though initially it no doubt was shocking and odd because of its unconventionality. Its sheer superiority, however, led to a cultural shift in not only high-jump technique but also corresponding aesthetic response. Let this be a lesson. As with many things we come to prize as beautiful, it was an acquired taste.

Notes

1 Sibley is often interpreted as embracing supervenience about aesthetic properties, although see MacKinnon (2001: 82) for a rejection of this interpretation.
2 Mumford (2012: 25–7, 29) provides a convenient overview of this progression.
3 See particularly Best (1978: 199–22).
4 Cordner (ibid.: 301–2) also cites Wulk (1979) and Kupfer (1975) as exponents of functionality accounts similar to Best's.
5 In the case of strength, see Lacerda (2011).
6 This extreme position I am responding to appears to be held by Edgar (2013a: 80), for whom sport aesthetics should give way to a hermeneutics of sport. But I take these as complementary rather than competing approaches.

References

Best, D. (1978) *Philosophy and Human Movement*, London: George Allen & Unwin.
Cordner, C. (1984) 'Grace and Functionality', *British Journal of Aesthetics, 21* (4): 301–13.

Cordner, C. (2003) 'The Meaning of Graceful Movement', *Journal of the Philosophy of Sport*, *30* (2): 132–43.

Davis, P. (2001) 'Issues of Immediacy and Deferral in Cordner's Theory of Grace', *Journal of the Philosophy of Sport*, *28* (1): 89–95.

Edgar, A. (2013a) 'The Aesthetics of Sport', *Sport, Ethics and Philosophy*, *7* (1): 80–99.

Edgar, A. (2013b) 'The Beauty of Sport', *Sport, Ethics and Philosophy*, *7* (1): 100–20.

Hohrod, G. and Eschbach, M. (de Coubertin, P.) (2000) 'Ode to Sport', *Olympic Review*, *26* (32): 29.

Holt, J., Holt, L. E. and Pelham, T. W. (1996) 'Flexibility Redefined', in T. Bauer (ed.) *Biomechanics in Sport* (Vol. 13), Thunder Bay: Lakehead University, pp. 170–5.

Hume, D. (2002) 'Of the Standard of Taste', in T. E. Wartenberg (ed.) *The Nature of Art: An Anthology*, Orlando: Harcourt, pp. 39–47.

Kupfer, J. (1975) 'Purpose and Beauty in Sport', *Journal of the Philosophy of Sport*, *2* (1): 83–90.

Lacerda, T. (2011) 'From *Ode to Sport* to Contemporary Aesthetic Categories of Sport: Strength Considered as an Aesthetic Category', *Sport, Ethics and Philosophy*, *5* (4): 447–56.

MacKinnon, J. (2001) 'Heroism and Reversal: Sibley on Aesthetic Supervenience', in E. Brady and J. Levinson (eds.) *Aesthetic Concepts: Essays After Sibley*, New York: Oxford University Press, pp. 81–99.

Mumford, S. (2012) *Watching Sport: Aesthetics, Ethics and Emotion*, New York: Routledge.

Sibley, F. (1959) 'Aesthetic Concepts', *Philosophical Review*, *68* (4): 421–50.

Wulk, N. G. (1979) 'A Metacritical Aesthetic of Sport', in E. G. Gerber and W. J. Morgan (eds.) *Sport and the Body: A Philosophical Symposium* (2nd Ed.), Philadelphia: Lea and Febiger, pp. 340–4.

3 Performer aesthetics

Sport aesthetics tends to focus on observers, on what it's like to appreciate athletic beauty from the sidelines, whether one is witnessing a live event or watching a recording of it. However, it is also important to consider individual athletes themselves, a performer's own perspective on what she is doing. A beautiful movement can be appreciated not only by those watching but also by those performing it. In other words, athletes can be not only objects but also *subjects* of aesthetic appreciation. Athletes who perform beautifully have a different but relevant and privileged point of view on what they do, on the aesthetic value they create, embody, and realize. In this chapter we turn to athletes' aesthetic experiences of their own performances. (I use the term 'performer' here to broaden the implied scope – you can appreciate your own kinetic beauty outside a sport context – and acknowledge that some of the material I will draw from was originally concerned with dance rather than sport, though it applies no less to the latter.)

To avoid confusion, let me be clear that I am not speaking of athletes who are adopting an observer's perspective in appreciating a performance aesthetically, as when watching a play from the bench, or even on field when not directly involved in a play, or even when they really *are* involved but find pleasing not their own but an opponent's or teammate's efforts apart from their own. Nor am I speaking of an athlete who observes a recording of her performance with a critical eye. No, it is a performer's aesthetic response to one's own movements while doing them that is my focus here, the seemingly paradoxical – but actually simply dual – role of being both agent and audience, creator and critic, of one's athletic efforts. This is no more paradoxical than an artist being pleased by his own works, with one individual occupying two normally but not necessarily distinct roles. There are complications to consider, as when one appreciates a group dynamic – a set piece, say – when one is clearly involved but only partly responsible for what is achieved aesthetically (and otherwise). In such cases it is a collaborator's appreciation of beauty, even if the result is spontaneous rather than planned.

Skillful play

A useful access point for aesthetic experience from the performer's perspective is via the concept of play. In broaching this subject, we must be careful to distinguish two broad senses of the term, which I call the *activity* sense and the *attitude* sense of play. What determines play in the former sense is the type of activity rather than the attitude of participants. Think of sports and other games. To participate in a game is to play it, and you are playing, in the activity sense, however seriously you take it and however much is riding on it. In this sense you play hockey no less as a professional vying for the Stanley Cup than in a backyard game of shinny. Your attitude has no bearing on whether your participation is play in the activity sense. By the same token, no attitude adjustment, no lighthearted approach or playfulness, can transmute certain activities into play in the activity sense. However much fun you may have as a neurosurgeon, for instance, this is not an activity that you can play, although you may pretend to do it without really doing it, or, in other words, play *at* it, as children play doctor.[1]

When it comes to play in the attitude sense, however, what makes something play or not is wholly a matter of the participant's attitude. If a participant's attitude is playful, if she derives a measure of lighthearted fun from the activity, then she is at play in the attitude sense. As the attitude sense of play stands independent of the type of activity itself, it follows that *any* activity – however serious – can constitute play in the attitude sense. In this sense serious activities such as brain surgery, practicing law, and aviation may constitute play (as may less beneficial activity like crime), at least for some people in certain cases. Whether such attitudes are acceptable from a moral standpoint is another matter and depends on both the nature of the activity and whether the play element is consistent with, detracts from, or enhances one's performance. This is true to a certain extent in sporting domains, where playful attitudes are generally more encouraged.

Since play in the attitude sense varies across and even within individuals, it is in this way relativistic, and so the same activity may count as both playful to one subject and nonplayful to another owing to the different attitudes involved. When one is playing in this sense, a significant part of one's motivation is intrinsic. Even where one engages in a sport for instrumental reasons like maintaining good health, the heart of one's playful attitude is valuing the activity for what it is, for its own sake. Other sorts of intrinsically valuable activity, such as behaving morally, may be valuable for their own sake irrespective of fun and pleasure – doing the right thing often isn't particularly fun – but the intrinsic value of a sporting activity to a player will be found precisely in the enjoyment they find in it: a subjective rather than objective sense of intrinsic value. This is not to say that any activity so valued will necessarily count as play, but an activity provides those who value it intrinsically with a kind of pleasure in which such value partly consists.

Of course an activity can be pleasurable without being *aesthetically* pleasurable, as when one appreciates a nude painting exclusively for erotic stimulation. But there is a kinship between the play attitude appropriate in sport and the playful attitude appropriate in the arts. We may see play in both domains, following Hyland, as a kind of 'responsive openness' to situations, partly chaotic, partly ordered, and that athletes and artists at their best employ a spontaneous creativity to navigate (1990: 117). This is different from the dull, unresponsive, and unplayful pleasures of satisfying basic biological needs. The gourmand's pleasure is not the gourmet's. Just as an artist may appreciate aesthetically the beautiful work he is in the process of bringing into the world, so too may an athlete appreciate, from the inside, the graceful movement, the elegant routine, the pretty play, the stunning performance, she is bringing into the world.

Creating art and playing sports can be fun to do even with fairly low levels of skill, barely enough even to count as *doing* one or the other. However, merely taking pleasure in such activity need not be aesthetic. It might well constitute, again, a basic sort of pleasure, an unrefined joy of movement, akin to the basic pleasures of eating, drinking, and so on, as if I were to take pleasure in an in-process poem or a sport movement not as a response to its emerging quality but because it is *mine* and not someone else's. The pleasure may not be ordinary, however, to the extent that the type and quality of the activity – the writing or the playing – are appreciated for what they are, for their own sake, as *abstractable* from the subject. If I were to find the result pleasing irrespective of who performed it, then my response has a greater claim to being aesthetic. This refinement tends to increase in proportion to the artist's or athlete's skill level. Not only are art and sport domains of skill; they are both domains in which one can appreciate aesthetically the exercise of domain-specific skills. All else being equal, the greater the skill level in question, the more its exercise is aesthetically appreciable by both observers and the agent himself. So unbiased artists will be able to appreciate the exercise of skillful creativity in themselves and other artists, and likewise unbiased athletes will be able to appreciate the exercise of athletic skill in their own and in their opponent's case. In the individual's own case, the more her skill is appreciated as *skill* and not just *hers*, the more plausible that any resulting pleasure, even if self-generated and -concerned, is aesthetic in character. It is at this level that one can also appreciate aesthetically one's skill in competition with comparably skilled opponents. Part of this pleasure may be personal, a proper pride in such achievement, but the latter, the achievement itself, takes precedence. Pointless self-assertion is neither particularly moral nor particularly aesthetic.

Being in the zone

In any domain of skilled activity, including various work activities, accomplishing suitable tasks suitably well, performing at one's best, is associated with a certain state of mind and body which in sports contexts is sometimes called *being in the zone*. Philosophers of sport have been mostly interested in such phenomena, aptly enough, from a phenomenological perspective (e.g., Breivik 2013).[2] This is understandable, of course, but if any value considerations enter the discussion, it is only peripherally in the guise of data to be explained, a seemingly descriptive account of what it's like for athletes, from their perspective, when they are playing particularly *well*. The quality of performance is assumed, but the normative dimensions of the experience itself are otherwise marginalized. Given what I have said earlier, however, such quasi-descriptive accounts of being in the zone obscure one of its essential elements. In my view, being in the zone is not just having the right 'body-mindset' to play particularly well, because the pleasure of that body-mindset has a decidedly aesthetic quality (and not just because body movements generate sensations that are termed 'kinaesthetic').[3]

To see this, consider Csikszentmihalyi's notion of flow, which models peak experiences in skilled domains. Flow is 'a state of consciousness where one becomes totally absorbed in what one is doing, to the exclusion of all other thoughts and emotions' (Jackson and Csikszentmihalyi 1999: 5). Beyond sharp focus on one's immediate undertaking, flow also brings a particular kind of enjoyment, 'a harmonious experience where mind and body are working together effortlessly, leaving the person feeling that something special has occurred' (ibid.). Situationally, flow comes from the right balance between the challenge of the activity and the skills and abilities one has to meet that challenge (ibid.: 16), as well as other markers including having a feeling of control and loss of self-consciousness and doubt (ibid.: 26–7). Such peak experience and peak performances tend to go together, and though they are the very realizations of the best an athlete can give to or get from a sport, they do not guarantee competitive but only a kind of personal success.

Again, in the phenomenology of sport these experiences are invariably examined without regard for their aesthetic dimension.[4] Indeed, in Jackson and Csikszentmihalyi's *Flow in Sports* (ibid.), the terms 'aesthetic' and 'beauty' do not appear in the index at all, and 'art' sporadically appears only to indicate one type of skill domain in which flow experiences occur. In a way this is surprising, since the notion of flow as a special kind of harmonious experience fits snugly into a long-standing tradition in aesthetic theory dating back arguably to Aristotle. Typical experience is dull, conflicted: you want to do something but ought to do something else, try to do something but find the task uninteresting or too daunting. The heart of aesthetic experience, however, is not conflict but harmonious resolution, what I elsewhere call *resolutive* experience.[5] As distinct from ordinary, boring experiences, flow likewise involves an intense, harmonious response to ongoing activities, a resolution of conflict not only between mind and body but also, in the psychological realm, between the intellect and the emotions, which on my account is precisely what constitutes aesthetic experience. Thus we can and should conceive of flow as the active counterpart to more passive or contemplative forms of aesthetic experience.

One possible objection to interpreting flow aesthetically comes from the notion that peak performances are associated not with a special kind of experience but rather with a more or less unconscious state of automatic receptivity and responsiveness. In other words, peak performance is a product not of some corresponding experiential peak in contrast to normal consciousness but of its inverse, an experiential *valley*, as if in a way one is sleepwalking to success. This view is associated with the work of Hubert Dreyfus (e.g., Dreyfus and Dreyfus 1986) and, up to a point, admittedly, this just-do-it view, as Barbara Montero dubs it, is somewhat plausible. Not only do experts have automated skills that demand greater attention by nonexperts, but also extraneous thinking and awareness can certainly interfere with performance.[6] Still, though, the automaticity of basic skills and bracketing unhelpful thoughts and irrelevant stimuli suggests, and is compatible with, the focused attention involved in flow and aesthetic experience.[7] Not minding irrelevancies does not preclude but rather fosters the essential specialness of the aesthetic.

Another objection to an aesthetic interpretation of flow may derive from a traditional but restricted view of aesthetic experience. On such a view, aesthetic experience requires the subject to distance themselves from the object of appreciation, to give it a disinterested attention so as to value it for its own sake (e.g., *not* being erotically stimulated by the nude painting). Traditional aesthetics is thus associated predominantly with vision (and to a lesser extent hearing) and with rare experiences afforded by museums and other places discontinuous with everyday life. Flow experiences, however, are characterized not by impersonal distance from, but rather by personal *immersion in*, the appreciated movement. An implication of this traditional view is that aesthetic experiences of sport, assuming they are even possible, are the portion of fans and not athletes as well, since the latter are too close to the appreciated object for disinterested attention. On a more contemporary, pragmatist view, however, aesthetic experience is continuous with everyday life, standing out as a more complete, coherent, and intense form of otherwise common, less satisfying experiences (Dewey 1980: 36–7, 43).[8] Thus it might be *easier* to achieve aesthetic experience as an active participant of a given activity than as a mere passive observer (unless one is lacking in requisite skills, in which case sideline appreciation will be easier than performance). I conclude that an aesthetic reading of flow is both useful and defensible.

Proprioceptive aesthetics

Traditionally, the five senses are not accorded equal importance as potential sources of aesthetic experience. Basic pleasure in what is naturally agreeable may be obtained through any one sense modality as well as combinations of sense modalities, but not aesthetic pleasure on a traditional view. The same tradition extending through Kant that construes aesthetic experience as needing psychological distance, naturally enough, is associated with the more general tendency of many philosophers to privilege vision and to a lesser extent hearing over the other senses. Thus vision, which obviously allows us to access visual art, counts as an aesthetic sense, as does hearing, for it gives us access to music, spoken verse, and certain aspects of theater. Touch may allow us to appreciate the textural qualities of sculpture, but its status is lower still, although perhaps not so low as taste and smell, which are more basic, animalistic, and, on the traditional view, lacking the right sort of fine-grained discrimination and psychological distance. It is only relatively recently that the fine-grained discriminations of, say, oenophiles and gourmets have been taken seriously by philosophers as suggesting the potential of these modalities as legitimate aesthetic senses. An aesthetic sense, in this sense, provides access to the right sort of properties – whether aesthetic or aesthetically relevant – to provide for aesthetic experience.

The five senses do not provide an exhaustive list, however. There is also proprioception, the internal sense of one's own body position as well as its orientation in and movement through space. Proprioception is important both in itself and arguably, as phenomenologists would urge, as a foundation for embodied consciousness generally. It may also be an aesthetic sense. Indeed, for vigorously championing proprioception as a bona fide aesthetic sense, Montero may deserve credit as the vanguard of *proprioceptive aesthetics*. For Montero, 'proprioception is an aesthetic sense [such] that one can make aesthetic judgments based on proprioceptive experience' (2006: 231). Expert dancers can proprioceive the 'beauty, grace, and other aesthetic properties' of their movements; technical changes might be motivated because they *feel* 'more exciting, or graceful, or brilliant', and so on (ibid.). Similar considerations apply *mutatis mutandis* to athletes, whether they compete in aesthetic sports where such feedback is crucial for performance, or in purposive sports where it matters far less. Of course, proprioception is not *predominantly* an aesthetic sense (nor is any other modality), nor is it the only source of feedback for a dancer. Visual feedback is also important (in studio mirrors, for instance), as is verbal feedback from choreographers, aural input from accompanying music, and so forth.

Perhaps the most intriguing part of Montero's position draws on the hypothesis of mirror neurons, which are specialized in the following suggestive way: they fire when subjects register a certain kind of action, irrespective of whether they observe another doing it or they are doing it themselves.[9] Such neurons might facilitate empathetic kinaesthetic responses when movement is seen rather than performed. On this view, we register movement proprioceptively even if we are witnessing someone else perform it. As Montero sees it, we have not merely visual and auditory responses to dance performances we observe but also proprioceptive responses, which means in effect that we can proprioceive *another's* movements (2006: 238).[10] This coheres with Montero's related argument that being an accomplished dancer oneself is liable to enhance one's capacity to judge dance aesthetically (2012). If proprioception informs the experiential and evidentiary bases provided by observation, refinements in proprioceptive sensitivity via practice and performance, all else being equal, would yield corresponding refinements in judgment.

Against Montero, and in league with David Best (1974: 142), Graham McFee staunchly opposes the notion that being a dancer has any bearing at all on one's ability to artistically judge dance, expertise in either domain being irrelevant to the other (1992: 273). The very same would seem to hold in sport, where being an elite athlete and being, say, a kinesiology professor appear entirely unrelated skill sets – I'm living proof – even if these skill sets pertain to the same sphere of activity and are found combined in rare individuals. More to the point, McFee rejects the very idea of a proprioceptive aesthetics. Taking proprioception to be a type of perception at all, much less as a basis for judging dance, is for McFee neither useful nor defensible, as in dance 'insofar as there is any perception at all, the perceptual modality is *visual*' (2011: 188). Since it is vision that ultimately constitutes *the* sensory modality for appreciating dance, it either trumps, or gives more precise content to, or is the standard for measuring, proprioceptive feeling. Likewise, even if proprioception were conceded to be a form of perception, it would provide no basis for *artistic* judgment of dance, since dance is an artistic domain that demands *understanding* (as opposed to mere feeling) (ibid.: 199). So even if proprioception did everything Montero claims, it would not bear on what McFee sees as our proper interest in dance as an artform (e.g., understanding *Swan Lake*, not knowing what it feels like to dance in a production of it).

Despite the trenchancy of McFee's critique, a proprioceptive aesthetics such as Montero envisions can be defended on most points. We can concede that there is no necessary connection between performative and critical expertise without having to deny the possibility of *contingent* connections in some cases (e.g., a particular theorist's performance background enhancing his theoretical acumen, as may be true of Montero herself, once a professional ballet dancer). Sure, critics with a performative background may be biased in ways that cast a more positive light on their own careers. Hockey pundit Don Cherry comes to mind here. But just as critics may ossify attribution bias on the basis of practical experience, so too may others do so from the ignorance of *lacking* such a background: the armchair quarterback phenomenon. Practical experience may deepen one's appreciation for observed achievements and so, by extension, one's justification for pronouncing judgment on them.

By the same token, if we admit that vision is the primary appreciative modality in dance, this does not imply that there are no other, even if lesser, appreciative modalities, as if there can be only one. Texture is primarily a tactile property, but this does not mean it cannot be accessed or appreciated visually along with or apart from tactile perception. Montero is surely right to say that dancers often appreciate what they do proprioceptively, as it must be where visual feedback is simply unavailable (as on stage, without the aid of studio mirrors). Montero argues, moreover, that nonvisual aesthetic proprioception is illustrated by blind dancers and that visual aesthetics, even in appreciating something so paradigmatically visual as the *Mona Lisa*'s smile, depends at least partly on proprioceptive resonance and not purely vision (2006: 235–6). Note that vision is sometimes overruled by bodily perception, as when touch confirms that a stick that appears bent when half-immersed in water is actually straight. Again, even if our 'proper' interest in dance is as an art whose works we seek to appreciate by understanding them, this does not imply that it is not *also*, relevantly, an appropriate place to seek aesthetic appreciation as well as understanding in both artistic and nonartistic forms. Finally, if proprioceptive aesthetics is irrelevant to artistic understanding, it follows that the latter is likewise irrelevant to proprioceptive aesthetics.

Where McFee's critique of Montero concerns the very idea of proprioceptive aesthetics, mine concerns specifically the highly speculative claim that one can proprioceive other people's movements. (In general, I find proprioceptive aesthetics along Montero's lines quite promising.) I agree that watching rather than performing certain movements may nonetheless resonate in our proprioceptive systems. Indeed, it is a long-standing trope of boxing movies – dating back as far as 1949's *The Set-Up* if not earlier – for fans to get so caught up in the action that they start to mimic the activities in the ring, throwing punches, ducking, and so on, as if the pugilistic exploits were their own. But to have a proprioceptive response to something does not imply proprioceiving it, not just because the response might be erroneous but, more pertinently, even if it is correct. One analogy here is with touch. Having a tactual response to something not touched but merely seen (as in seeing a familiar texture, for instance), having the stimulus register or represented in one's tactual system, does not imply touching it. To a certain extent in such cases the imagination may be involved, but in any event the conceptual limits of such perceptions as belonging to at most a single subject are clear. Far from merely stretching the concept, Montero's proposal, interpreted strictly rather than polemically, goes too far.[11] This, however, is a local criticism. For recognizing the importance of bodily perception, proprioceptive aesthetics in general is not only viable itself but also coheres well with basic commitments in the philosophy of sport.

Notes

1 Indeed, in the spirit of Huizinga (1950: 8), we might add a third sense of 'play': play as make-believe.
2 One can imagine a Heideggerian text on *in-der-zone-sein* (being-in-the-zone).

3 It is a pity that 'kinaesthetic' pertains to sensations of body movement generally, since the term might otherwise designate, more narrowly, the aesthetic appreciation of one's own movements.
4 This connection was suggested in conversation with Darren Kruisselbrink.
5 This sense of 'resolutive' is elaborated in Holt (1996: 427). For how this account complements neuroaesthetics, see Holt (2013: 4–5). See also Holt (2015).
6 See also the extreme classic view of Herrigel (1981) and, more limitedly, Holt (2003: 136).
7 For a sustained critique of just-do-it in favor of what she calls cognition-in-action, see Montero (2016), reviewed in Holt (2017).
8 For a Deweyan account of running as aesthetic experience, see Martin (2007: 175–7). See also Elcombe (2012) for an argument for applying pragmatist aesthetics to the philosophy of sport.
9 Montero (2016: 201) cites a literature review by Rizzolatti and Craighero (2004).
10 Montero is aware of courting paradox here, although she understates the fact: 'Although this is extending our use of the term "proprioception", I suggest that it is legitimate' (ibid.). I will return to this point.
11 In her more recent book Montero introduces scare quotes to formulate her account: 'observers can "proprioceive" a dancer's movements' (2016: 201).

References

Best, D. (1974) *Expression in Movement and the Arts*, London: Lepus Books.

Breivik, G. (2013) 'Zombie-Like or Superconscious? A Phenomenological and Conceptual Analysis of Consciousness in Elite Sport', *Journal of the Philosophy of Sport*, *40* (1): 85–106.

Dewey, J. (1980) *Art as Experience*, New York: Perigee.

Dreyfus, H. L. and Dreyfus, S. E. (1986) *Mind Over Machine: The Power of Human Intuition and Expertise in the Era of the Computer*, New York: Free Press.

Elcombe, T. L. (2012) 'Sport, Aesthetic Experience, and Art as the Ideal Embodied Metaphor', *Journal of the Philosophy of Sport*, *39* (2): 201–7.

Herrigel, E. (1981) *Zen in the Art of Archery*, New York: Vintage.

Holt, J. (1996) 'A Comprehensivist Theory of Art', *British Journal of Aesthetics*, *36* (4): 424–31.

Holt, J. (2003) *Blindsight and the Nature of Consciousness*, Peterborough: Broadview Press.

Holt, J. (2013) 'Neuroaesthetics and Philosophy', *SAGE Open*, *3* (3): 1–7.

Holt, J. (2015) *Meanings of Art: Essays in Aesthetics*, Montreal: Minkowski Institute Press.

Holt, J. (2017) Review of Barbara Gail Montero, *Thought in Action: Expertise and the Conscious Mind* (Oxford: Oxford University Press, 2016); *Metapsychology Online Reviews*, *21* (10), http://metapsychology.mentalhelp.net/poc/view_doc.php?type=book&id=7829, accessed 23 January 2019.

Huizinga, J. (1950) *Homo Ludens: A Study of the Play Element in Culture*, Boston: Beacon Press.

Hyland, D. A. (1990) *Philosophy of Sport*, Saint Paul: Paragon House.

Jackson, S. A. and Csikszentmihalyi, M. (1999) *Flow in Sports: The Keys to Optimal Experiences and Performances*, Champaign, IL: Human Kinetics.

Martin, C. (2007) 'John Dewey and the Beautiful Stride: Running as Aesthetic Experience', in M. W. Austin (ed.) *Running and Philosophy: A Marathon for the Mind*, Malden, MA: Blackwell, pp. 171–9.

McFee, G. (1992) *Understanding Dance*, New York: Routledge.

McFee, G. (2011) *The Philosophical Aesthetics of Dance: Identity, Performance and Understanding*, Hampshire: Dance Books.

Montero, B. G. (2006) 'Proprioception as an Aesthetic Sense', *Journal of Aesthetics and Art Criticism*, 64 (2): 231–42.

Montero, B. G. (2012) 'Practice Makes Perfect: The Effect of Dance Training on the Aesthetic Judge', *Phenomenology and the Cognitive Sciences*, 11 (1): 59–68.

Montero, B. G. (2016) *Thought in Action: Expertise and the Conscious Mind*, Oxford: Oxford University Press.

Rizzolatti, G. and Craighero, L. (2004) 'The Mirror-Neuron System', *Annual Review of Neuroscience*, 27: 169–92.

4   Design matters

In Chapter 1 I offered a five-level analysis for sport aesthetics, and since then the focus has been implicitly on Levels 2 and 3, that is, on individual athletic movements and overall performances, whether appreciated by observers or by the performing athletes themselves. It is time now to consider in greater detail Level 4, that of the framework(s) in which athletic movements make sense as such, without which they would appear capricious if not irrational. Often part of the aesthetic appeal of a sport movement or performance depends on the framework that makes it possible. Perhaps the most important of these frameworks is that expressed by the rules of a given sport, whose design in terms of artificial constraints in essence *creates* these activities qua sports. Gamewrights, who create and modify the rules, are influenced by various design considerations in tailoring rules to make for a good or better game. Thus here I turn to matters of design that matter aesthetically to the appreciation of sport, including not only game design and distinctions among different types of games, but also, briefly toward the end, other design and framework influences such as venue architecture, uniform and equipment design, and mediated spectatorship.

Principles of design extend beyond purely aesthetic considerations, of course. They also include pragmatic concerns of feasibility and functionality. Thus sometimes whether something is well designed might be a matter of performing a certain function rather than eliciting aesthetic experience, whereas in other cases aesthetic factors predominate and supersede functionality, or constitute perhaps an impractical kind of functionality – that of producing aesthetic experience.[1] However, although aesthetic and functional design may be at odds, they can otherwise converge where 'form follows function' in functionalist aesthetics. Although it may be far from clear how to disambiguate 'function' in such contexts (Winters 2007: 41), functionalist aesthetics certainly has its advocates in fields from anatomy to architecture. In what follows my focus is principally on design aesthetics much as it may, and I think does, intertwine with the constitutive and moral elements of sport.

Game design

The classic account of games in the philosophy of sport proposed by Bernard Suits highlights the importance of rules for defining what games are and, by implication, the aesthetic properties they have. Suits defines playing a game as 'the voluntary attempt to overcome unnecessary obstacles' (1973: 55). These unnecessary obstacles are artificial constraints imposed by rules on attempts to achieve an objective, which Suits calls *pre*lusory in that it is describable without citing the rules.

Suits's full definition is the following: 'To play a game is to attempt to achieve a specific state of affairs (*prelusory goal*), using only means permitted by the rules (*lusory means*), where the rules prohibit use of more efficient in favor of less efficient means (*constitutive rules*), and where such rules are accepted just because they make possible such activity (*lusory attitude*)' (ibid.). Suits is a formalist about games in taking the rules to define them, from which it follows that illegal play fails to count as playing the game at all.

Gamewrights create the initial frameworks for game-play, grounding what it can become in fact, including aesthetic properties of the play. The beauty of a slapshot, for instance, depends on the rules of ice hockey that allow it as a legitimate move the execution of which might have a certain aesthetic value as well. It is not just explicit rules that may be tailored for partly aesthetic reasons of what would make for an enjoyable game to play or watch. Conventions governing the application of rules may also be informed by aesthetic considerations (Mumford 2014: 184). The officials may impose rules less strictly to maintain game flow, a partly aesthetic motivation. But the account currently dominant in philosophy of sport is neither formalist nor conventionalist but interpretivist, according to which a sport should be understood as given by our best interpretation of the rules in connection with the internal goods of the practice, the game's gratuitous logic. On such a view too not only moral but also aesthetic values shape our understanding of what sport is and ought to be (Torres 2012: 299).

Regardless of any specific theory of the relationship between sports and their rules, then, those involved in game design broadly conceived, those who write, modify, apply, and interpret rules, may be guided by partly aesthetic considerations of what would make for a good or better game.

Mumford calls this 'the aesthetic hypothesis: that *aesthetic considerations are essential to the being of sport and continue to shape its development*' (2014: 183, original emphasis). Elliott says, 'those who determine what the rules of a game are to be have a responsibility to safeguard the possibility of the emergence of beauty' (1974: 113–4).[2] According to Holowchak, likewise, because sports fundamentally are about athletic excellence, not just winning, ' "excellence" itself implies that there is an ineliminable aesthetic component to sport. Sport is excellence principally because sport is beautiful' (2000: 45). It should be clear by now that I also endorse the aesthetic hypothesis, though this book is not predicated on it, as sport would stand as an important source of aesthetic pleasure even if aesthetic norms were excluded from our best interpretation of sport. Part of my motivation is to counterbalance undue marginalization of aesthetic concerns in much philosophy of sport literature – especially in ethical debates fueled implicitly by aesthetic norms – and part of the reason is to account for variability in preferences for certain types of sports and certain styles of play. Many sport preferences are informed by unconscious responses to the very aesthetic features of activities that shaped their design.

Sport preferences are not entirely arbitrary or irregular, however. Indeed, some sports are more popular than others. If we take the world's most popular sport, it is obvious that the design appeal of this activity resonates with a great number of people far beyond idiosyncratic or niche preferences – not that there's anything wrong with those. It is partly for socioeconomic reasons that football (soccer) is the world's most popular sport; it's cheap and widely accessible. But the moniker 'the beautiful game' is no accident or mere honorific. Soccer also has aesthetic appeal that is literally global in scope. A small part of the reason is that, like many though not all sports, soccer has discernible appeal on all levels of the stratified aesthetic analysis proposed in Chapter 1: physique, movement, performance, framework, and significance. More than most other sports, however, soccer has a worldwide cultural significance in large measure, I believe, because of the aesthetic potency of its unique framework provided in the letter and spirit of its rules. Something about soccer's very framework makes it for very many more beautiful than any other sport. This needs explanation even if we dispute, as we might, the judgment of preeminence.

Most soccer fans would be quick to enumerate features of the game they find particularly appealing: the skills, the tactics, the creativity, the overall dynamics, and the drama of the game. All of this, however, obscures by assumption soccer's structural framework – on which its aesthetic appeal depends. If anything in soccer is a constitutive rule, it is that one may not use one's hands. If a player picks up the ball and runs downfield American football style, that person is not playing soccer. Of course there are exceptions: throw-ins and ball handling by goalkeepers, but even in the latter case there are limits on where and when hand use is allowed. Why does this matter? Here's why. The thing about human hands is that they coevolved with the human brain and are, in effect, the outward anatomical expression of what makes us unique. Frank Wilson: '[A]ny theory of human intelligence which ignores the interdependence of hand and brain function, the historic origins of that relationship, or the impact of that history on developmental dynamics in modern humans, is grossly misleading or sterile' (1999: 7). Since game rules are artificial constraints on legal play, the quintessential physical game would be one that virtually rules out the outward physiological expression of human distinction: the hands.³ For this reason, soccer is plausibly a quintessential physical game, the paradigmatic sport. This doesn't imply that it should be everyone's favorite or rule out the possibility that other hand-restrictive games could achieve competing emblematic status.⁴ But what it does suggest is that, in severely limiting what legally might be done with the hands, soccer represents, more than any other popular physical game, what it is for an activity to *be* a game at all, and in this resides an important part of its aesthetic appeal.

Types of sport

It is not just the unique frameworks of individual sports that are aesthetically relevant. At a more abstract level, commonalities uniting various sports into groups or types are also relevant. Along with its uniquely appealing characteristics, for instance, soccer shares more abstract constitutive and aesthetic commonalities with other ball sports, team sports, time-regulated sports, purposive sports, and – at the sociocultural level – international sports, (sometimes) Olympic sports, and so on. Like each sport, each sport type also has characteristic aesthetic elements, and there appears to be some variation in how one both divides the relevant subtypes and consequently decides on the appropriate taxonomy for aesthetic analysis.

One relevant distinction is that between what Kretchmar calls T games and E games; the former are regulated by a span of *time* (e.g., hockey's three 20-minute periods), hence T games, the latter by a certain number of *events* (e.g., baseball's nine innings), hence E games (2005: 38–9).⁵ On Kretchmar's account, relative to E games T games are aesthetically flawed because they encourage stalling, as when a team is ahead in the score and reverts to a more defensive strategy, resulting in a duller game (ibid.: 40). This position might seem odd if one considers that many of the world's most popular sports, many of them team ball sports, including soccer, are T games. (As celebrity culture illustrates, however, being flawed and being popular are entirely consistent. One could argue that certain flaws fuel the popularity of some celebrities and some sports alike.) Mumford argues, on the contrary, that the time limits of T games mirror those of life itself, which enhances the dramatic potential of T games as reflecting our mortality and counts as an aesthetic virtue rather than a vice (2012: 24). Although different preferences are clearly evinced here, it is not clear how much purchase either has on aesthetic judgment.

So who, if either, is right? Observe first that delays occur in E sports too and may qualify as a comparable aesthetic flaw. How many times with a runner on first will a pitcher *not* pitch to the batter and opt to attempt a pickoff or a batter step out of the batter's box to adjust equipment or otherwise delay the proceedings? This is reflected somewhat curiously in Kretchmar's choice to illustrate the aesthetic flaws of stalling: hypothetical cases from golf (2005: 40), which is an E game. Often in E games time limits will be imposed to minimize the number and extent of these delays; one is not permitted to stand over the golf ball or at the service line in tennis indefinitely. Even if this fails to reduce the number of competitive encounters between opponents (unlike the stalling in T games), it remains a kind of irritating delay for players and fans alike. On the other hand, this kind of tension may fall in line with Mumford's position as enhanced drama even if it is otherwise a flaw. As for Mumford's view, even if T games mirror our mortality, they do so in a decidedly *dis*analogous way. We do not typically know in advance when the buzzer of life will sound; much less do we watch the countdown clock in nervous anticipation. If anything, E games better reflect human mortality in coming to an end at some till-then indeterminate time. Yes, in T games one aims to beat the opponent *and* the clock, which increases the overall challenge and in this sense might also enhance the spectacle. This may however indicate nothing more than mere preference for different types of drama. Just as some people prefer realistic to romantic literature or cinema, where neither genre is necessarily superior, so too may T and E games realize at their best different types of athletic beauty appealing to different types of taste. Perhaps in some ways the aesthetic draw of these different types of sports resides partly in their very flaws.

Another, more fundamental distinction in sport aesthetics is that originally articulated by David Best between purposive and aesthetic sports

(1974). We have encountered this distinction already, characterizing purposive sports as those where aesthetic properties like grace fail to bear on performance outcomes and aesthetic sports as those where such properties do figure into determining performance outcomes. In purposive sports like hockey, swimming races, or track, outcomes are determined by who has the most goals, the fastest time, and so forth, whereas in aesthetic sports like figure skating, synchronized swimming, and gymnastics, style counts in the determination of the scores by judges who are looking for athletes to achieve both technical difficulty and good form or artistic impression. This distinction, though drawn on different bases, corresponds roughly to that proposed by Suits between game and performance sports (1988: 17). On Kupfer's threefold distinction, aesthetic or performance sports are termed qualitative/formal sports, with purposive sports subdivided into two distinct types: quantitative/linear sports, where the outcomes depend on measurement (how much, how fast, how far), and – in a narrow sense – competitive sports, in which opponents struggle to impede each other in vying for the game's objective (1988: 392–4).

These distinctions among sports foreground different types of aesthetic and aesthetically appreciable properties.[6] In directly competitive sports, where opponents actively struggle against one another, the aesthetic potential is thereby enhanced in certain respects. Joseph Kupfer: 'The complications introduced by human opposition multiply the aesthetic possibilities in competitive sports – dramatic possibilities due to social interaction' (ibid.: 396). Mumford, on the other hand, sees it in the increased importance of strategy and the abstract patterns of play that consequently emerge (2014: 186). I think both are on to something here, yet neither goes deep enough, perhaps because they have in mind team ball sports like soccer as paradigms.[7] Observe that strategy and social dynamics, though still important, matter much *less* in individual competitive sports and in team events without balls or similar projectiles. The enhanced aesthetic of competitive team ball sports, I submit, is owing not just to social dynamics or strategic patterns but, more basically, to the joint complexity and unpredictability of projectile behavior and group response. The chance for surprise and sudden reversals of fortune both locally and in contests as a whole helps explain the enhanced aesthetic of such head-to-head competition.

In those sports variously designated aesthetic, performance, qualitative, or formal, again different aesthetic properties come to the fore. Thus graceful style becomes less of by-product of some successful performances than a *requirement* for competing at all. As I argued in Chapter 2, it is not just that grace becomes more prominent in aesthetic sport than in purposive sport; rather, its very realization takes on a different character, that of efficiency in approximating ideal forms rather than the fluidity of movement that suggests grace in purposive sports. More than anything else it is the prominence of formal properties of movement and, by extension, of the physique of the athlete as well that lends aesthetic sports so readily to being well represented, and somehow even captured, in photography and other static media. I believe this reflects a deeper distinction, originating in Kant, between free and dependent beauty. For Kant, dependent beauty depends on bringing about a certain end, whereas free beauty is pleasing in a purely formal way irrespective of realizing any end (2005: 48–9). I maintain that the aesthetic appeal of purposive sports counts as dependent beauty in a Kantian sense, defined in terms of realizing the purpose of the activity. An attempt on goal typically will not be beautiful unless it succeeds or stands a good chance of succeeding; a nice move may not deceive the defender, but a beautiful deke must. But the appeal of aesthetic sports realizes a kind of free beauty in Kant's sense, as illustrated by cliff diving for instance, in being aesthetically appreciable for its own sake apart from any competitive context.[8] This indicates a need to qualify my earlier claim that sport frameworks create artificial skills and aesthetic properties. The natural, formal, free beauty of movement in aesthetic sports transcends the constraints of competitive context or consideration of any practical end, unlike, say, the grace of a powerful running stride, whose aesthetic appeal depends on functionality inside or outside a sporting domain.

Consider last those purposive sports that do not involve the direct dramatic confrontation of competitive sports in Kupfer's sense or the beauty-forward scoring of aesthetic sports. In such quantitative/linear sports the winner is determined by completing a racecourse the fastest, lifting the most weight, jumping or throwing the greatest distance, and so forth. As Mumford sees it, in such events success correlates with aesthetic value, 'because speed, form, extension, suppleness, power, strength, and so on, as well as being those [properties] that contribute to athletic success, are those we also admire aesthetically. Why exactly this should be is a matter we can leave to the specialist aestheticians' (2014: 186). We should be cautious, however, because in these sports success frequently issues from techniques that disturb rather than please the aesthetic sensibility: Jesse Owens's odd long-jump landing, Nancy Gulbis's dipsy-doodle golf swing, Emil Zátopek's untidy running, Seabiscuit's eggbeater gait, among numerous examples. The real mystery is how we can appreciate such performances aesthetically alongside their often more stylish yet inferior competitors. One answer is that there are at least two different kinds of appeal here: the aesthetic of style and what may be called the *factual* aesthetic of raw achievement. That a human being (or horse in Seabiscuit's case) is capable of such feats is itself a thing of beauty. Another related answer, which I will revisit in Chapter 6, is that our aesthetic stance should be more open than it tends to be, our attitude more inclusive, our sense of value pluralistic.

Other designs, other frames

As a springboard to briefly address further aesthetic features of framework and design, consider another picture painted by Mumford: 'In football, the lush green grass upon which two teams in beautifully designed contrasting kits play against a spectacular backdrop of colourful and noisy fans, hosted in an architecturally pleasing stadium, all make it an extraordinary experience to the senses . . . a markedly aesthetic experience' (2014: 184–5). One important facet of the framework highlighted here is the *physical setting* in which a sport activity occurs. Beyond the emphasis on venue architecture and presence of a crowd, however, the mention of lush green grass implies an outdoor stadium. For outdoor sports weather plays a significant part in facilitating or hampering a good game together with an enjoyable viewing experience. Indeed, in truly outdoor sports it is hard to overestimate the importance to aesthetic appreciation of good weather overarching other features of the natural and built environments: the mountainside for skiing, the links for golf, the waterway for boating, the cityscape for marathons, and so on.

The more the physical setting is artificial rather than natural, obviously, the more certain considerations of design come to the fore, from the formal and evocative symmetry of Beijing's National Stadium to the quirky significance of Boston's Fenway Park. In some cases it might be hard to distinguish Level-4 formal appeal from Level-5 significance. The symmetrical appeal of Beijing's National Stadium is tied to its resemblance to a bird's nest, to having been built for the 2008 Summer Olympics, to it serving as the backdrop for landmark events (such as Usain Bolt's record-breaking performance in the 100 meters), and so on. In other cases it is easier; the close-looming asymmetry of Fenway Park's Green Monster may offend a formalist's sensibility, but for fans this quality may be compensated for by Red Sox franchise history. Similarly, one may appreciate the colors and tailoring of official athletic uniforms and logos, though distinguishing that from the known significance attached to the designated team is hardly straightforward. Note this mix in Simon Critchley's recollection of a particular soccer viewing experience: 'I want Juventus to win because I have always loved their black and white striped shirts and the defensive resilience of their play' (2017: xv). Other times it is easier to tell, for instance when you are not invested in either the team or the sport and simply like the uniform. The aesthetics of design is also relevant in considering the equipment and related apparatus athletes use, whether the functional appeal of seemingly aerodynamic design or more decorative details such as the classic pentagram-panel or some alternative soccer ball design.

Design also clearly informs one of the most powerful framing devices in modern sport in the form of electronic and digital media. The technological frames of media broadcasts, for better or worse, are even infiltrating live spectatorship far more than mere scoreboards, PA announcers, organ music, and the like, which are more traditional and less intrusive parts of the physical and cultural frame for spectator sports. Plausibly the most noticeable symptom and most apt symbol of this phenomenon is the jumbotron, which may be meant to complement but actually *competes* for attention with the on-field activities, as does the cellphone, which too many people choose to mediate even their live experience of sporting events. Notice how watching televised or Internet broadcasts implies that only some varieties of sport, at usually more elite levels and only certain matchups at that, are worth watching, because only some are broadcast, invariably for financial reasons. That such framing, by design if not intent, can limit and skew our general and aesthetic interest in sport we ignore at our peril. I will revisit this topic in Chapter 6.

Thus, framing informs not only which aspects of the wide world of sports we take to be significant but also the very significance we attach to them, which straddles the Level 4/Level 5 distinction. Nowhere is this more apparent than in the history of sport institutions, which frame sport performances in and judge their significance relative to specific sociocultural narratives. In this way the evolution of sport institutions and media proceed in parallel, each reflecting and informing the other. Consider Jesse Owens's gold medal and record-setting performances at the 1936 Berlin Olympics, particularly as framed by Leni Riefenstahl's *Olympia* (1938) in a manner that captures and grounds their manifold significance both in and beyond the history of sport. In the next chapter, then, I turn to aesthetic significance.

Notes

1 For a such functionalist account of art, see Iseminger (2004).
2 On this point see also Elcombe (2012: 206).

3 Some may suggest other candidates, such as the feet, as being no less distinctive, which would undermine my argument.
4 Although I played varsity soccer in high school, in some ways I preferred the nonstandard court game 'soccer squash', which I played with my father.
5 The designations 'T games' and 'E games' do not appear until later.
6 Here I follow Mumford (2012: 22) in following Kupfer (1988).
7 Kupfer distinguishes competitive sports from individual sports (ibid.: 392–3), although various individual sports like boxing, tennis, fencing, and many others would count as competitive in his narrow sense.
8 Cliff diving would be beautiful even if there were no such thing as diving competitions, though a beautiful body check or slapshot, say, would not make sense or seem beautiful if there were no such thing as a hockey game.

References

Best, D. (1974) 'The Aesthetic in Sport', *British Journal of Aesthetics, 14*: 197–213.

Critchley, S. (2017) *What We Think About When We Think About Soccer*, New York: Penguin.

Elcombe, T. L. (2012) 'Sport, Aesthetic Experience, and Art as the Ideal Embodied Metaphor', *Journal of the Philosophy of Sport, 39* (2): 201–7.

Elliott, R. K. (1974) 'Aesthetics and Sport', in H. T. A. Whiting and D. W. Masterson (eds.) *Readings in the Aesthetics of Sport*, London: Lepus Books, pp. 107–16.

Holowchak, M. A. (2000) '"Aretism" and Pharmacological Ergogenic Aids in Sports: Taking a Shot at the Use of Steroids', *Journal of the Philosophy of Sport, 27* (1): 35–50.

Iseminger, G. (2004) *The Aesthetic Function of Art*, Ithaca: Cornell University Press.

Kant, I. (2005) *Critique of Judgment*, J. H. Bernard (trans.), New York: Dover.

Kretchmar, R. S. (2005) 'Game Flaws', *Journal of the Philosophy of Sport, 32* (1): 36–48.

Kupfer, J. H. (1988) 'Sport – The Body Electric', in W. J. Morgan and K. V. Meier (eds.) *Philosophic Inquiry in Sport* (2nd Ed.), Champaign, IL: Human Kinetics, pp. 390–406.

Mumford, S. (2012) *Watching Sport: Aesthetics, Ethics and Emotion*, New York: Routledge.

Mumford, S. (2014) 'The Aesthetics of Sport', in C. R. Torres (ed.) *The Bloomsbury Companion to the Philosophy of Sport*, London: Bloomsbury, pp. 180–94.

Riefenstahl, L. (1938) *Olympia* (The Leni Riefenstahl Archival Collection), Venice: Pathfinder Home Entertainment.

Suits, B. (1973) 'The Elements of Sport', in R. G. Osterhoudt (ed.) *The Philosophy of Sport: A Collection of Original Essays*, Springfield: Charles C. Thomas, pp. 48–64.

Suits, B. (1988) 'Tricky Triad: Games, Play, and Sport', in W. J. Morgan and K. V. Meier (eds.) *Philosophic Inquiry in Sport* (2nd Ed.), Champaign, IL: Human Kinetics, pp. 16–22.

Torres, C. R. (2012) 'Furthering Interpretivism's Integrity: Bringing Together Ethics and Aesthetics', *Journal of the Philosophy of Sport*, *39* (2): 299–319.

Wilson, F. R. (1999) *The Hand: How Its Use Shapes the Brain, Language, and Human Culture*, New York: Vintage.

Winters, E. (2007) *Aesthetics and Architecture*, London: Continuum.

5 Aesthetic significance

Suppose you are watching a recorded performance of an athlete on the uneven bars. It appears to be going well despite the difficulty of executing each movement and transitioning to the next, all while maintaining good form and realizing ideals of line, grace, rhythm, and poise, all capped by a high dismount and perfectly stuck landing with no hint of waver. A remarkable performance, a beautiful performance, yes, but that is not all. It occurs in competition, in front of a large crowd, and not just any competition or crowd but those suggesting an international meet. Further still, suppose the judges echo the crowd's applauding sentiment by awarding the routine a perfect ten, the first ever at this level, and that the gymnast – Nadia Comaneci – would earn a total of seven such scores on her way to three gold medals at these 1976 Montreal Olympics. As we saw in the previous chapter, the historical and institutional framing of sport substantially affects its significance, and, as this Comaneci example shows, the significance of sport performances may influence our aesthetic judgments of them. If we could somehow bracket our visual impression of Comaneci's perfect 10 performance from its significance, we would no doubt find it beautiful, but not nearly *as* beautiful. Aesthetic judgment is informed as much by understanding as it is by sensory input. In this chapter, then, I turn to Level 5 in addressing different types of significance that affect our aesthetic appreciation of sport.

One clear source of aesthetically relevant significance in sport is the athlete's physique. The athleticized body, which in my five-level analysis constitutes a level in its own right, Level 1, also links with aesthetically relevant significance at Level 5. We hazard oversimplification in seeing the athletic body as one that is lean, muscular, flexible, capable, and skilled, only because conditioning the body for different capacities and skills required for different sports can result in radical physical differences: the ectomorphic marathoner versus the meso-endo weightlifter, for instance. It may be hard for an occidental observer to appreciate that the characteristic physique of, for instance, a sumo wrestler is no less built and trained to its tasks than the decathlete's. But in general an athleticized body is often seen as signifying at least the kind of work ethic required to build and fine-tune it, if not also an indication of moral virtue besides, as seen through the lens of ancient perspectives on the value of sport.[1] We tend to see lean, muscular bodies prejudicially as being physically capable and skilled, as indicating capacity and prowess, both in concert with and even irrespective of performance. The hyperathletic bias implicated here is a matter to defer to the next chapter, which will be devoted entirely to the question of aesthetic biases.

Corporeal significance aside, in this chapter my focus is principally types of significance that are relevant to sport aesthetics and that have some standing or presence in the philosophy of sport literature. The list is inclusive. First on the list is the question of whether sport qualifies as drama in any important sense, a question of psychological significance beyond the bare fact that sport is something people care about. Next is the issue of potential interaction between aesthetic and moral values, specifically whether the moral significance of an athlete's performance may in some cases affect its aesthetic value. In the third section I address a distinction that has received very much play in the sport philosophy literature, that between purist and partisan approaches to sport spectatorship, which I frame partly in terms of different views of aesthetics in sport and the types of significance permissibly attached to sporting events. Alongside the more familiar figures of the purist and the partisan, I also identify various other dramatis personae lurking in the wings that complicate the picture of sport spectatorship more than the simple purist/partisan distinction would suggest. The picture that emerges is one of aesthetic pluralism.

Drama and representation

To see sport as a possible source of drama is to ascribe to it a kind of psychological significance whereby one cares not only about the box score but also about watching the contest as it unfolds toward those eventual results, even in the case of a recorded game where one already knows the result. Typically, though, a sporting event takes on dramatic significance, when it does, because the outcome is forthcoming but as yet uncertain. Uncertainty of outcome is one ingredient. That is part of the reason why lopsided competitions and blowouts often have little drama; even if the conclusion is not foregone, the uncertainty of the outcome is substantially diminished at least on a psychological level. Appreciating the uncertainty of result in more competitive matches builds psychological tension, another element of drama, a tension that depends not only on uncertainty of outcome but also on the observer being invested in that outcome and how it is unfolding. This does not necessarily imply that one has bet on the outcome or otherwise chosen sides, but it does imply that observers are swept up in the proceedings. With unfamiliar or uninteresting sports, of course, one can recognize that an event has dramatic significance for others without caring about or sharing in the drama oneself, much less in the release of such tension at the denouement – the third facet of drama. Whether a sporting event has dramatic significance, then, rests on *someone* being caught up in the action, but not necessarily everyone.

In the philosophy of sport literature, the question of whether sport provides some kind of drama is often raised in connection with other questions, only some of which are germane to my discussion. Many thinkers regard the drama question in light of whether sport can be considered an artform. Keenan, for instance, argues that sport counts as not only dramatic but also as a tragic artform (1975). Best, on the other hand, cautions against inferentially slipping from the fact that we use words like 'drama' and 'tragedy' in talking about sport to the position that sport exhibits these attributes in the same way that the drama and tragedy of theatrical performances do (1978: 117). Mumford counters Best in arguing that the drama of sport and the drama of theater are less clearly distinct than Best's argument implies, with the result that 'there are some closer parallels between art and sport' than are usually thought in a Bestian vein (2012c: 56). Culbertson (2017) gives a detailed critique of Mumford's account in effectively defending Best's hardline position. One important consideration in this debate is whether anything in sport is comparable to the sort of imaginary object or representational content we find in theatrical art. In addressing the drama question I am likewise concerned with the possibility of sport as representation, though I am not concerned with the further question of the possible artistic status of sport, a topic to be addressed in Chapter 9. Having dramatic significance and representational content is neither necessary nor sufficient for art. As illustrated by certain abstract paintings and news reports, some art is neither dramatic nor representational, and some dramatic representations are not art.

Best elaborates his take on the sport-as-drama question to draw an analogy with the error of supposing that, because sport is occasionally beautiful and otherwise aesthetically rewarding, it is also art: 'A similar misconception occurs with respect to the terms "dramatic", "tragic", and their cognates. . . . [I]t certainly cannot be assumed that they are used in other contexts as they are in art' (1978: 117). The key distinction for Best is 'the convention that tragedy in a play happens to the *fictional characters* being portrayed, and not to the actors' (ibid., original emphasis). By contrast, we have 'no comparable convention in sport such that it would makes sense to say of a serious injury in Rugby that it occurred to the full-back, but not to the man who was playing full-back' (ibid.: 118). The principled difference consists in the fact that in the theatrical arts, though not in sport, 'the object of one's attention is an *imagined object*' (ibid., original emphasis) or, in other words, the fictional characters and events theatrically represented by actors on stage. When we use the term 'tragic' in describing sports, then, we may be referring to serious injury or using it 'in the irritatingly prevalent but barbarously debased sense' of athletic failure (ibid.: 119), not the thrill of victory but the agony of defeat. The upshot on Best's view is that if we can speak of drama and tragedy in sport at all, they are not of the same conventional, fictional, desirable kind that we find in theatrical art.

Where Best sees the drama in sport as paling next to the robust drama of the theater, and perhaps only a secondary, derivative version of the latter, Mumford prioritizes the real drama of sport and everyday life over the merely imagined drama of the theater. At the same time, though, he seeks to blur without denying them the distinctions Best draws between artistic and sportistic drama and between art and sport themselves. 'Sport contains', Mumford says, contra Best, 'what for all the world looks like drama' (2012c: 50). Against the idea that sport bears some superficial resemblance to unscripted theater, Mumford claims that the rules of sport provide it with certain commonalities to *scripted* theater, in telling us how the event is to proceed, when the game ends, and so forth (ibid.: 51). Finally, on Mumford's account we can speak of a distinction between an athlete qua person and her athletic role comparable to that between an actor and her dramatic role (ibid.), the implication perhaps being that although the drama of sport is somehow *more* real than true theatrical drama, there remains a sense in which the drama of sport is still *less* real than that of everyday life.[2] Overall, we are to see sportistic and artistic drama, as well as sport and art generally, to be less sharply distinguished than is usually thought.

In a detailed criticism of Mumford's criticism of Best, Culbertson is careful to enumerate the various threads of Mumford's argument, even if it is not entirely clear how they are meant to weave together (2017: 4). Culbertson is right to insist, contra Mumford, that there is no plausible reason to view sport as akin to scripted theater and that the roles played by athletes and the roles played by actors are usually too dissimilar to cut against Best's distinction between the imagined characters represented in artistic drama and the real on-field players in sportistic drama (ibid.: 5–7). Indeed, the rules of sport are too open in restricting rather than determining athlete behavior to correspond even loosely to a script in which what is said and done and how it is to be said or done – and who if anyone 'wins'! – is specifically prescribed even if actors under directors have certain degrees of latitude in bringing their performances to stage.[3] The rules of sport by contrast may both suggest dramatic structure and structure dramatic events, but they constrain rather than provide the resulting narrative content. Even in the unscripted theater of improv, participants are supposed to work together toward a common goal rather than competing against one another for an unshareable victory. Likewise, trying to ascribe agency to athletic roles rather than to athletes themselves is, with certain exceptions perhaps, either procrustean or toothless in that, to return to Best's example, after the match in which the fullback is injured it is still the person who played fullback who requires medical attention.

Nonetheless, I think that Mumford is onto something important in seeing commonalities between artistic and sportistic drama, even if it is mistaken to privilege either of them, as Best and Mumford severally do, as the predominant (for being the more real or robust) type of drama. This commonality may be seen in the thumbnail sketch of drama with which I began this section, the psychological tension and building to an uncertain if inevitable denouement predicated on an observer's interest in the unfolding of that outcome. A complementary point from Keenan is that 'athletic contests involve drama. Dramatic tension is created when athletes are able to overcome the limitations placed on freedom through superlative action' (1975: 39). This sense of drama, a decidedly psychological sense, is apparently shared by sports fans and theatergoers alike and is in no way touched by Best's talk of the conventions of drama as a theatrical genre. I thus offer a hard distinction between drama in a psychological sense (drama as something *felt*) and drama in a generic sense (drama as something *made*). Conventional drama on my account is admittedly a different way of bringing about psychological drama than in sport, but this is entirely consistent with the psychological feeling of drama – getting caught up in the unfolding of the proceedings – proving similar or even the same in the two domains. One may object that sport is a less reliable means than the theater to generate drama or that sportistic unlike artistic drama strictly depends on outcomes that are *not* predetermined. Both points may be true, but they amount only again to differences in implementation. It may also be observed, however, that we may be overestimating conventional drama's rate of success as well as underrating sport's batting average in producing psychological drama. Likewise, psychological drama can be produced in an observer regardless of whether the outcome is unknown, as with unfamiliar stage plays and live sporting events, or known, as with familiar plays and rewatched recordings of sporting events.

By the same token, the undeniable and principled difference between the fact that artistic drama is created by design whereas sportistic drama almost always emerges spontaneously from unscripted if partly planned and strategized activities means neither that conventions of artistic drama are excluded from sport nor that sport cannot lend itself to representational interpretation. Even if Best is correct that in *most* cases we cannot distinguish the person of the athlete from the role they play, this does not mean that there are *no* such cases. In figure skating, for instance, we sometimes distinguish between the athlete and the conventionally dramatic role she is playing. At the end of Katarina Witt's *Carmen* program from the 1988 Calgary Winter Olympics, Witt's eponymous character, as she does in Bizet's opera, dies – though Witt herself lived on to receive the gold medal. Such a distinction is certainly atypical of sport, as Best's view suggests, but it is nonetheless mistaken to view artistic conventions as wholly removed from sport drama.

More important, when Keenan suggests that there are theoretically interesting parallels between sport and theatrical tragedy, he is aware that sport tends to lack the intentionally created representations that are found in figure skating. For Keenan, just as theatrical tragedy does, sport can build dramatic tension and yield emotional catharsis, with outcomes that involve recognition (of what one has done or failed to do) and reversal (of advantage or fortune), and where defeat is explicable by some 'fatal flaw' because of which one is unable to overcome the challenge (1975: 49).[4] Again, though, Best would insist on the fact that in sport what we lack is precisely the sort of designed representation that we enjoy in the theater. But mimesis, the representation of life in art, goes both ways. As Keenan puts it, '[t]he mimetic feature of athletic tragedy lies partially in its portrayal of life in microcosm' (ibid.: 45). Further, 'tragedy seems to be an essential element in our universe. . . . The athlete who is second best symbolizes both excellence and failure' (ibid.: 51), and as embodying 'the universal athlete' (ibid.: 48) thereby also represents human beings in general in striving and inevitable defeat. Such representations are not *created* as such as in art or as Best requires but are instead *discovered* in or fittingly *ascribed* to athletic contests. Nothing, furthermore, prevents our either finding in or ascribing to sport such symbolic significance even though the events are not predetermined by artistic design.[5] In this way the dramatic significance of sport may be tied implicitly to its potential symbolic value. We can admit this without having to maintain implausibly that sport is literally tragedy or that the psychological drama it promotes is not realized in a substantially different way in the arts.[6]

Aesthetic–moral interaction

We often think aesthetic and moral values to be entirely distinct. For instance, that a person is or has done something beautiful has no bearing on whether she is a good person or has done something morally praise-worthy. Likewise, being plain or ugly may be a misfortune, and yet it has no bearing on the moral status of one's deeds or character. To position morality and aesthetics in this way as distinct, autonomous realms of value is sometimes called *autonomism*, and it is hard to deny that in most cases, most domains, autonomism appears justified and by extension should be the default position in cases of uncertainty. In other words, if autonomism has exceptions, we would require sufficiently strong reasons to accept them and to qualify the principled distinction accordingly.

Sport appears to be one domain in which moral significance may, and sometimes should, affect one's aesthetic judgment. 'Factors that are ethi-cally bad can detract from sport's aesthetic value', according to Mumford, 'and factors that are ethically good can enhance sport's aesthetic value' (2012c: 68). Since aesthetic considerations likewise inform a game's design and gratuitous logic, the influence goes both ways, so 'the best way to characterize the relationship between the two is therefore in terms of *interdependence*' (ibid.: 76, original emphasis). As a result Mumford is a champion of what I call the interdependence thesis.[7] Despite the relative breadth of this view, however, most of Mumford's discussion concerns how immorality, specifically immoral content, character, or context, can taint otherwise beautiful performance.

I should mention that although Mumford's focus is specifically on sport, some of his key examples come from outside that domain. Take for instance his discussion of Leni Riefenstahl's *Triumph of the Will* (1934), an artistically significant propaganda film that was commissioned by the Nazis to document and glorify the Nuremberg rallies. Mumford echoes a critique by Devereaux (1998) according to which the morally repulsive content of the film substantially undermines its artistic merits. No ques-tion, we would infer that something was seriously amiss with someone who was able to dispassionately appreciate the film from a purely aesthetic point of view, that is, without the expected negative emotional response overwhelming any possible aesthetic pleasure. We could still maintain a kind of abstract autonomism, however, in allowing that the film is indeed a great work of art even if we should be unable to appreciate it as such while watching it. But that is not Mumford's approach, as he dismisses the apparent artistic merits of *Triumph of the Will* as 'superficial' (2014: 191), a verdict he extends to Riefenstahl's *Olympia* (1938), documenting the 1936 Berlin Olympics, whose elements of propaganda are far subtler than *Triumph*'s, yielding a film much easier to watch and appreciate. Whether Mumford is right about the Riefenstahl cases or not, art seems to be another domain in which aesthetics and ethics can be expected to interact, especially as the attitudes endorsed by works or the circumstances of creation and performance often *intrude* into the art itself and are of sufficient moral significance to outweigh or complicate any potential aesthetic interest.[8]

Still, this issue probably needs further elaboration to solve what I elsewhere call the *Nazi aesthetics problem*, an apparent implication of Mumford's position (Holt 2017: 76). This is akin to the Nazi data problem, that is, whether is it morally permissible to use data obtained from inhumane medical experiments.[9] Is it morally permissible to use Nazi aesthetics? The answer isn't entirely straightforward. We may rightly have moral compunctions against displaying Nazi insignia, for instance, but the matter is less obvious when we consider the SS uniforms, designed by Hugo Boss, or the silhouette of the Volkswagen Beetle (allegedly designed by Hitler), and so on. If Mumford is right about the aesthetic innovations of Riefenstahl's films being tainted, what of the use of such innovations by later filmmakers, like George Lucas in *Star Wars*? Perhaps the only thing wrong with Riefenstahl's aesthetic is that it was put in the service of the Nazi agenda. Inasmuch as this may seem a retreat into autonomism, however, note that the aesthetic *does* remain compromised in its original form; once more, while watching *Triumph of the Will* it would be wrong for us *not* to have our aesthetic response drowned out by moral repugnance.

Mumford's most persuasive examples from sport concern neither content nor context but rather character. For Mumford, if we discover that an impressive performance was the product of cheating, say, the cheater's character flaw will tend to diminish our aesthetic appreciation of that performance. Mumford's example is Ben Johnson, who at the 1988 Seoul Olympics appeared to win the 100 meters in a record 9.79 seconds, only to be disqualified soon afterward by failing a drug test. For Mumford, before the scandal broke, we admired Johnson's run 'in aesthetic awe', although afterward 'we no longer see it as having aesthetic value' (2012c: 73, 74). Now we might disagree that Johnson's performance, even on a presumption of innocence, merits aesthetic *awe* or, once the guilty verdict was in, that it failed to retain *any* of its original aesthetic value, but the point that the drug test failure hamstrings aesthetic response remains convincing.[10] On the other side of the divide, appreciating that an athlete's performance comes from virtue rather than vice is likely to enhance our aesthetic appreciation. Mumford's example here is England's most recent World Cup victory: 'To English football fans, that 1966 win was already a thing of beauty' (ibid.: 75). It was later revealed that team captain Bobby Moore had been at the time a cancer survivor; for Mumford, 'to discover that the character of the England captain was even better than we thought enhances [the game's] aesthetics even further' (ibid.). This, I suggest, is one facet of the aesthetic appeal of the underdog, perhaps along with a work ethic aesthetic, since theirs is a greater call to courage that, when answered, may achieve genuine poignancy.

Not all of Mumford's examples are equally clear or compelling, however. An example is his account of the Dynamo Kiev death match in World War II, where Kiev locals were forced to play an exhibition match against an occupying German side, with death as the price for victory.[11] 'There may have been some beauty and profundity in Dynamo nevertheless winning the game', Mumford says, but owing to the morally abhorrent situation, 'it was consequently not something knowingly we should have admired aesthetically' (ibid.). But, as I argue elsewhere (2017: 78–9), if the Dynamo team's play was beautiful and, beyond that, an expression of the players' courage, as helpless onlookers in the crowd aware of the dire consequences, we would be wrong *not* to be moved aesthetically by their play. This is elegantly illustrated by the film *Victory*, John Huston's fictionalized account of the death match, with an international team of Allied POWs (played by Pelé and Bobby Moore, among others) substituted for the Kievite side. The beauty of the Pelé character's goal-scoring bicycle kick is only enhanced by the deplorable circumstances. Similar considerations apply to the aesthetic power of Jesse Owens's Olympic achievements in 1936 in the heart of Nazi Germany as filmed by Riefenstahl and overseen by Hitler. Although some details and specific cases may remain subjects of dispute, the interaction thesis is still a plausible, provocative, and mostly unexplored topic worthy of sport philosophers' further investigation.

Purist, partisan, and other dramatis personae

Although Mumford's account of aesthetic–moral interaction has not yet received much attention in the philosophy of sport literature, the same cannot be said of his version of the purist/partisan distinction. 'A partisan', as Mumford defines them, 'is a fan of one particular sports team: and it usually is a team. Partisanship is rarer in individual sports' (2012c: 9). The latter claim seems to neglect the fact that individual sport athletes often represent groups (nations, regions, sponsors, schools, and other institutions) and are thus also members of teams, and so will appeal similarly to patriotic or local partisans – though this last point is a mere quibble. Partisans are emotionally invested in their team to the extent that they sacrifice objective values of good sport to a kind of tribalism. 'The purist', by contrast, 'is a fan of a sport, and may love deeply the sport concerned, but has no allegiance to any particular team' (ibid.: 10). According to my five-level analysis, the purist focuses on Levels 2, 3, and 4, the aesthetics of movements and plays and of performances and games, respectively, with little consideration of significance apart from such properties. The partisan, on the other hand, focuses on Level 5 and more specifically on that idiosyncratic kind of significance in which fandom consists. For partisans, when their team wins, it matters to them simply because it is *their* team. On Mumford's view, the partisan lacks the kind of psychological distance required to experience sport aesthetically, and would prefer his team to garner an ugly win than to perform beautifully but lose. The purist prefers beautiful play *simpliciter*, and it is for this reason that Mumford champions the purist as an aesthete with the right attitude to appreciate sport dispassionately.

We should note that the purist/partisan distinction originates in work by Nicholas Dixon, is drawn somewhat differently, and is often discussed with little regard for its aesthetic nuances. Although Dixon's conception of the partisan is similar to Mumford's, he understands the purist rather differently as one who 'supports the team that he thinks exemplifies the highest virtues of the game, but his allegiance is flexible' (2001: 149). Mumford thinks this gets the purist wrong, that true purism has nothing to do with allegiances to teams but rather allegiance to, if anything, the sport itself and the best it has to offer (2012c: 14). Discussions of the distinction that follow Dixon rather than Mumford tend to neglect or sideline aesthetic considerations, focusing instead on the internal goods of sport practices in either general or ethically valenced terms.[12] Mumford therefore deserves credit for aestheticizing the distinction, for drawing attention to its import for sport aesthetics in a way both intuitively grounded and theoretically useful.

It would be overly simplistic to hold that in watching sport one is either a pure purist or a pure partisan, even assuming that these categories exhaust the types of sport spectatorship. Many of us occupy the middle ground somewhere along the spectrum between these two extremes. As a champion of purism, Mumford nonetheless posits a trade-off between the aesthetic detachment of purism and the emotional engagement of partisanship (2012a) and the possibility that we can oscillate between the two perspectives in the course of a single athletic event (2012c). It is small wonder, then, that several philosophers recommend a subtle blend of purism and partisanship to optimize spectatorship: Dixon's moderate partisan (2016: 233), Feezell's moderate purist (2013: 89), Davis's deep partisan (2019: 255), and so on. Such middle-ground hypotheses are plausible, yet despite differences among them amount, at some level of abstraction, to the same theoretical move. There are other moves, however, that we should seriously consider.

One prospect proposed by Russell (2012: 24) is that there is no single ideal kind of sport spectatorship. In the spirit of such pluralism we should notice that just as one can be too much of a partisan in denying other teams their due, supporting sides that are unapologetic cheats, and so on, one might also be an excessive purist in appreciating sport movements merely in an abstract, formalist way irrespectively of the rules or competitive context. This may be feasible in the case of aesthetic sports, as we saw in Chapter 4, but this would not be appropriate in sport generally or even in appreciating aesthetic sports as such in any real depth. We would ignore the significance of such performances as Comaneci's in Montreal that make them not just lovely or impressive to look at but aesthetically powerful. Admittedly, the partisan *might* be unduly biased in comparing his team to its opponents, but when the partisan is *not* so biased it seems he has a claim to aesthetic experience comparable to that of the purist. Where the purist has the detached experience required by Kantian aesthetics, the partisan can at least sometimes have the engaged experience celebrated by Deweyan aesthetics. The purist and partisan might therefore represent not different attitudes toward sport's aesthetic rewards but different legitimate *types* of aesthetic experience – another point for pluralism.

So much discussion concerns the purist/partisan distinction that one is likely to think that these are the only possibilities. As Culbertson rightly observes, however, 'there seems no reason to think that partisan and purist ways of watching sport are the only options' (2015: 191). This is a point of substantial weight. On Culbertson's view, alternatives to the purist's aesthetic interest and the partisan's emotional interest include taking an interest in sport as a spectacle, as a source of drama and tension, as providing a sense of community, or culture, or identity (ibid.: 192).[13] One may well argue that these proposed alternatives fail to realize the substantial promise of the point they are meant to illustrate, because they are too easily subsumable by the very distinction they are meant to de-dichotomize. As we have seen, for instance, both the partisan and the purist may experience the psychological drama provided by sport. Likewise, feeding into a fan's sense of identity or community is part of partisanship's appeal. Still, even though such motives may be consistent with purism or partisanship, they do not necessarily imply either and so may count as genuine alternatives after all.

We can further develop Culbertson's insight by realizing, first, that though the partisan's pleasure need not be, it may also be or involve aesthetic pleasure to the extent that fans can find their team's performance to be beautiful and to value it at least partially for that reason – even if we suspect their verdict to be biased. This is not Culbertson's position, since he seems to follow Mumford's apportioning of aestheticism to the purist (ibid.: 184) just as he insists along Bestian lines that sportistic drama is not strictly aesthetic at all (ibid.: 192).[14] Mumford himself, however, admits that the partisan's reward may be partially aesthetic: again 'To *English football fans*, that 1966 [World Cup] win was . . . a thing of beauty' (2012c: 75, added emphasis). If we take seriously the notion that the purist and partisan can take different kinds of aesthetic interest in sport, other aesthetically relevant attitude distinctions will be thrown into sharp relief.

As the purist and partisan disagree about whether to take an aesthetic interest in sports or whether such interest should be detached or engaged, here are some other distinctions among the dramatis personae in the stands of sport spectatorship (see Table 5.1): whereas the traditionalist judges the merit and the beauty of sport against that of the past, the modernist measures the past against the standard of the present; the idealist judges

Table 5.1 Some aesthetically relevant attitude distinctions

Attitude distinction	Point of dispute
Purist vs. partisan	Aesthetic (dis)interest
Traditionalist vs. modernist	Historical yardstick
Idealist vs. pragmatist	Normative priority
Monist vs. pluralist	Variability of approach
Libertarian vs. paternalist	Degree of control
Elitist vs. amateurist	Best of sport
Work ethicist vs. play ethicist	Value source
Naturalist vs. technophile	Artificiality

sport against a conception of what it ought to be, whereas the pragmatist more forgivingly judges in terms of the status quo (among relevant subtypes here are the *aretist* – after the Greek '*arete*' – who privileges excellence over winning, versus the Lombardian, who inverts this order; and the Lockean, who values cooperative virtues such as sportsmanship, versus the Machiavellian, who perversely values successful rule-bending and -breaking as beautiful); the monist presupposes and thus favors a single optimal technique or strategy, whereas the pluralist prefers a more individually tailored and varied set of approaches; the libertarian prefers a hands-off approach to regulating sports, whereas the paternalist sees the interests of sport fostered rather by instituting appropriate controls such as bans on performance-enhancing drugs; the elitist finds most appealing sport at the very highest levels of achievement, whereas the amateurist valorizes sport in less institutionalized, more grass-roots forms; the work ethicist finds more pleasing and rewarding those grinding performances that stem from a strong work ethic, whereas the play ethicist (*ludist*?) finds beautiful those that flower as more creative and playful; the naturalist and the technophile likewise disagree over whether certain technological advances or retreats will detract from or enhance sport's aesthetic appeal.

This list is meant to be inclusive rather than exhaustive, terminologically arbitrary to a certain degree, and to describe spectrums akin to that between extreme purism and extreme partisanship. There are other aesthetically relevant distinctions that could be included, and those listed could be described in other terms. One worry here could be that some of these distinctions are seemingly assimilable to the purist/partisan distinction interpreted suitably broadly (i.e., with the purist representing objectivity, the partisan subjectivity, in the broadest possible sense). This concern has some merit. Consider, for instance, that the idealist's and pragmatist's attitudes may align nicely with those of the purist and partisan, respectively. However, one may perfectly well be a nonpartisan purist about sport *as it is* without necessarily thereby committing to some kind of unrealistic romanticism. Further, not every distinction appears so readily subsumable. It is not obvious, for instance, which if either of the traditionalist or modernist, or the monist or pluralist, has the better claim to purism. Further still, even if we could subsume all such distinctions under the purist/partisan distinction, identifying the partisan with various kinds of biases and the purist with the lack of such biases, the result would be useful, a finer-grained conceptual taxonomy for analyzing the purist/partisan distinction. But wherever such distinctions end up, some blendings, some extremes, will prove untenable biases, others permissible preferences, others still justified positions. The moral, unsurprisingly, is aesthetic pluralism.

Notes

1 On this point see any of many relevant works by Heather Reid (e.g., 2012).
2 This is my interpolation, although it seems condign to Mumford's view.
3 It should be clear for this reason that professional wrestling, as found in the WWE for instance, counts as a kind of theater rather than sport.
4 Unlike the fatal flaw of typical theatrical tragedy (e.g., Othello's jealousy), in sport this may be a morally neutral inadequacy (e.g., not being strong enough although one did one's best).
5 See also Welsch (1999: 223).
6 Kreft (2012: 228) proposes drama as the category on which sport aesthetics generally depends.
7 Many points in this section derive from Holt (2017).
8 For discussion and a middle-ground position on ethicism about art, see Wills and Holt (2017).
9 On the Nazi data problem, see Schafer (1986).
10 Insofar as we find Johnson's physique unappealingly *over*developed, this may inspire aesthetic arguments against performance-enhancing drugs in sport.
11 For a detailed account of the historical event, Mumford directs us to Dougan (2002).
12 Examples besides Dixon (2001) include Russell (2012) and Feezell (2013). Admittedly, Dixon (2016) does mention aesthetic motivations, but only in passing, not as a point of genuine interest. The notion of the internal goods of a practice derives from MacIntyre (1984: 187).
13 Russell (2012: 23) makes the related point that there are various purist/non-partisan reasons to watch sport: in hopes that the better team will prevail, to appreciate the exhibition of skills, or for pure entertainment.
14 The latter is an odd position, given Best's aesthetic/artistic distinction. Even if sportistic drama is different from artistic drama, that does not preclude appreciating the former aesthetically.

References

Best, D. (1978) *Philosophy and Human Movement*, London: George Allen & Unwin.
Culbertson, L. (2015) 'Perception, Aspects and Explanation: Some Remarks on Moderate Partisanship', *Sport, Ethics and Philosophy*, 9 (2): 182–204.
Culbertson, L. (2017) 'Purism and the Category of "the Aesthetic": The Drama Argument', *Journal of the Philosophy of Sport*, 44 (1): 1–14.
Davis, P. (2019) 'The Purist/Partisan Spectator Discourse: Some Examination and Discrimination', *Sport, Ethics and Philosophy*, 13 (2): 247–58.
Devereaux, M. (1998) 'Beauty and Evil: The Case of Leni Riefenstahl's *Triumph of the Will*', in J. Levinson (ed.) *Aesthetics and Ethics: Essays at the Intersection*, Cambridge: Cambridge University Press, pp. 227–56.
Dixon, N. (2001) 'The Ethics of Supporting Sports Teams', *Journal of Applied Philosophy*, 18 (2): 149–58.
Dixon, N. (2016) 'In Praise of Partisanship', *Journal of the Philosophy of Sport*, 43 (2): 233–49.

Dougan, A. (2002) *Dynamo: Defending the Honour of Kiev,* London: Fourth Estate.

Feezell, R. (2013) 'The Pitfalls of Partisanship', in *Sport, Philosophy, and Good Lives*, Lincoln: University of Nebraska Press, pp. 73–91.

Holt, J. (2017) 'Mumford on Aesthetic–Moral Interaction in Sport', *Journal of the Philosophy of Sport, 44* (1): 72–80.

Keenan, F. W. (1975) 'The Athletic Contest a "Tragic" Form of Art', *International Review for the Sociology of Sport, 10* (1): 39–54.

Kreft, L. (2012) 'Sport as a Drama', *Journal of the Philosophy of Sport, 39* (2): 219–34.

MacIntyre, A. (1984) *After Virtue: A Study in Moral Theory* (2nd Ed.), Notre Dame: University of Notre Dame Press.

Mumford, S. (2012a) 'Emotions and Aesthetics: An Inevitable Trade-Off?', *Journal of the Philosophy of Sport, 39* (2): 267–79.

Mumford, S. (2012b) 'Moderate Partisanship as Oscillation', *Sport, Ethics and Philosophy, 6* (3): 369–75.

Mumford, S. (2012c) *Watching Sport: Aesthetics, Ethics and Emotion*, New York: Routledge.

Mumford, S. (2014) 'The Aesthetics of Sport', in C. R. Torres (ed.) *The Bloomsbury Companion to the Philosophy of Sport*, London: Bloomsbury, pp. 180–94.

Reid, H. (2012) 'Athletic Beauty in Classical Greece: A Philosophical View', *Journal of the Philosophy of Sport, 39* (2): 281–97.

Russell, J. S. (2012) 'The Ideal Fan or Good Fans?', *Sport, Ethics and Philosophy, 6* (1): 16–30.

Schafer, A. (1986) 'On Using Nazi Data: The Case Against', *Dialogue, 25*: 413–19.

Welsch, W. (1999) 'Sport – Viewed Aesthetically, and Even as Art?', *Filozofski Vestnik, 20* (2): 213–36.

Wills, B. and Holt, J. (2017) 'Art by Jerks', *Contemporary Aesthetics, 15*: 1–8.

6   Aesthetic bias

I would like to begin this chapter with some reminiscences about one of my favorite sports, ice hockey. Like many born and raised in Canada, I learned the game early. I fondly remember as a youngster being taught to skate by my father on the frozen lake we were fortunate enough to live on, then countless games of shinny, organized games at the local rink, traveling for away games and tournaments. I recall my surname on the back of various jerseys and in the local newspaper listed among the house league scoring leaders one year. Another year I was honored by a team award for most sportsmanlike player. Limited as I was, I enjoyed some of my best moments on the ice, especially dekes, plays, and goals, and occasionally revisit them in my conscious mind as if in a personal highlight reel. Such experiences as a player were complemented in no small measure by spectatorship. Gretzky was in his prime, and I watched in breathless awe live broadcasts of many important moments in his career: scoring his 50th goal in 39 games in 1981, the Stanley Cup wins of the Oilers dynasty, and 1987's Gretzky-to-Lemieux Canada Cup–winning goal over the Soviet Union. After hanging up my skates, I continued playing vigorous and exhilarating road hockey games with high school friends. Though I no longer play and my viewership has waned significantly since my twenties, I still have a prized hockey card collection, including some Gretzkys in decent condition, though the gem of the collection is a mint(ish) Gordie Howe signed by Mr. Hockey himself when I met him briefly on the links at a local golf tournament.

What, you may ask, is the point of this skate down memory lane? Hockey clearly holds a personal significance for me, a significance that partly explains not only why it ranks among my favorite sports but also my aesthetic appreciation of it as a practice and the particular framework in which The Great One earned a soubriquet of such high respect and esteem. In a question, then, to what extent is my aesthetic appreciation for hockey over most other sports (and Gretzky over most other players) a matter of preference rather than bias? (As for providing a positive account of aesthetic judgment, I defer that to the next chapter.)

Preference or bias?

The pluralist conclusion of the preceding chapter raises the specter of sub-jectivism in a most rabid and unprincipled form, the idea that in aesthetic matters *anything goes*. There is a legitimate sense in which with matters of taste *chacun à son goût*, to each his own, but does this imply *de gustibus non disputandum est*, that there can be no dispute about taste? Yes and no. Perhaps my favorite sport is hockey and yours the marathon. We each like different sports the best. Is there any sense in which we have a real dispute here, some grounds for debate? Not unless we go further and try to assert our preferences as reflecting matters of fact or what one's judg-ment *should* be, if I took my preference for hockey to reflect a presumed fact that it *really is* the better sport and that you were therefore *mistaken* to prefer the marathon or believe that it is the superior sport. Obviously from an aesthetic standpoint each of these sports has relative advantages. The spectator-friendly dynamic of hockey is one of its aesthetic advantages, whereas the marathon has greater potential to symbolize sport as testing the limits of human endurance. But mere preferences, like yours for mara-thon, mine for hockey (or whatever), are untouched by objective differ-ences in value. If the marathon somehow proved, all things considered, to be the better sport, this fact by itself would not invalidate my preference for hockey. Divergent preferences are fine irrespective of objective value difference, if there is one. The exception of course would be cases where one's preference is for some morally objectionable activity, such as hunt-ing human beings for sport.

Assuming then that we are not dealing with preferences that are morally objectionable on their face, though a preference can be partly explained by appealing to a subject's background or context, and though it often doesn't need justification, this doesn't mean it lies altogether beyond justification. Part of what caused Gretzky to become my favorite hockey player is, no doubt, that I was exposed to him at a formative time for me during the height of his career. Consider David Hume's observation about literary art that 'we are more pleased, in the course of our reading, by pictures and characters, that resemble objects which are found in our own age and country, than with those which describe a different set of customs' (2002: 46). But I can nonetheless give good reasons for my preference, includ-ing the numerous records he still holds and embodying the best aspects of the game (as a multiple Lady Byng trophy winner, for instance), that not only provide justification for my preference where none is needed but also could be turned into a compelling argument for ranking him as the greatest and most beautiful to watch player in hockey history.[1] Such justifications, however, flirt with injustice in that they could dispose me to misjudge other great players, to deny earlier, contemporaneous, or later players their due. If my love of Gretzky inclined me to *slight*, say, a Bobby Orr, a Mario Lemieux, or a Sidney Crosby, that would indeed be blameworthy.

The key difference in matters of taste between innocuous preference (and possibly good judgment) on one hand and undue or malicious preference or judgment on the other comes down to whether the verdict in question is biased, much as this will often be a difficult matter to ascertain. In subsequent sections I will address some more common forms of bias and prejudice in sport cultures and subcultures that predispose subjects toward different forms of injustice, my focus being what I will call *aesthetic injustice*. Social injustice in various forms unfortunately is all too familiar to most of us and both affects yet is distinct from other forms of injustice. Some philosophers, for instance, identify different forms of *epistemic* injustice, often on the basis of a group prejudice (sex, race, and other marginalized groups), by denying members of such groups due regard for their concerns, perspectives, knowledge claims, arguments, and sense of reality.[2] By the same token, I propose we commit aesthetic injustice in sports by unfairly assessing either the aesthetic appeal of an athlete's efforts or the overall quality of their performance on the basis of irrelevant or problematic aesthetic criteria. If I deny the merits of Crosby's play because I am a Gretzky fan, that is, inclusively, an aesthetic injustice. If I summarily dismissed female athletes or women's sports as uninteresting, that would also be, though not merely, an aesthetic injustice. It would hardly be surprising to find someone's preference for men's sports to be rooted in more general sexist attitudes. One mark of acceptable attitudes and preferences, then, is avoiding such aesthetic injustice.

Technique and physique

Some of the more obvious forms of aesthetic bias in sport are embedded in more familiar forms of prejudice and discrimination in the culture at large. Yet I begin not there but with more sport-specific varieties of bias, although in a sense these too reflect, rather more dimly, wider cultural trends. On the one hand, in many sport subcultures is a tendency embrace a *homogenized* model, the notion that there is a single ideal technique, approach, or style for everyone, and on the other toward a *hyperathletic* model, the notion that the harder an athlete works, the more athletic they look, the better their sport performance. Despite the popularity and comfort of such assumptions in sport and fitness culture, though, they are in general and in many specific applications deeply flawed, as well as being entrenched, implicitly but insidiously, in aesthetic biases.[3] Simplicity is, all else being equal, both an epistemic and an aesthetic virtue, but even when all else is *not* equal, an aesthetic bias toward simplicity will often remain, as is evident in both the homogenized and the hyperathletic model. There is a parsimonious elegance in monolithic approaches, in the idea that every athlete should approximate the presumed ideal as best he or she can or that better athletes have worked harder and *look* the part more than their rivals.

The tendency toward homogenization of technique in sport in certain cases, especially in comparatively limited tasks and skills, may be warranted. In high jump, for instance, ever since Fosbury's invention of the flop, which has since proved the best among available techniques for elite competitors, the homogenization of technique seems justified. Even here, however, if some earlier technique – the scissor kick, say – had been presumed to be ideal, that presumption would inhibit experimentation with and development of new techniques such as the flop. As innovative for its time, too, the flop initially would have seemed an ugly, awkward, unusual technique. We now likewise may be aesthetically biased toward the flop and against further experimenting with yet newer possible techniques that, for all we know, could surpass or become a viable alternative to the flop. In general, the more complex or open the relevant skills and the competitive context, the more what counts as the best technique or approach will tend to vary across athletes (ibid.: 219). In golf, for instance, because of the wide range of physiological differences among elite players, we should see, will expect, and should appreciate both diversity of technique and idiosyncrasy of style (ibid.: 213). It is precisely in such cases, however, that we frequently find aesthetic bias toward classic approaches rather than openness to differences in personal style. Here the overly narrow, often too traditional, aesthetics of pundits and aficionado fans alike is liable to stifle the diversity embraced by aesthetic pluralism.

Considerations of functional success aside, such biases make sense, if they do at all, only in aesthetic sports where conforming to prescribed forms is part of what it means compete at all, to perform even basic movements, much less score well. The irony here, of course, as with many of the performing arts, is that achieving certain kinds of excellence may require not just training but overtraining, not just conditioning but punishing the body. Aesthetic biases, then, even built into the very fabric of sport itself, problematize it no less than in purposive sports. Note how the expectation of technical uniformity dovetails with expectations of certain kinds of physique vis-à-vis the hyperathletic bias, which has spilled over from fitness culture and sports into everyday life. True enough, many sports do tend to favor certain specific body characteristics. Champion distance runners will be lean and have exceptional cardiovascular systems. Champion gymnasts will be strong and flexible. Top decathletes will invariably look like athletes, but not necessarily top players in many sports: baseball, American football, golf, boxing, and even soccer. From the perspective of wanting our athletes to *look* athletic, 'the phenomenon of a Babe Ruth in baseball or a John Daly in golf is difficult to take' (ibid.: 217). Such norms have infiltrated the culture at large. We expect celebrities and people aspiring to be attractive generally to look no less athletic than stereotypical elite athletes. The hyperathletic bias, then, is inclusively harmful not only in sport subcultures. With this particular bias our culture has clearly gone too far.

We can therefore understand how different types of bias at Level 1 (physique) and Level 2 (technique) can skew our expectations and aesthetic responses to performance and style (Level 3) by mistaken ascriptions of significance (Level 5) to them as indicators of athletic prowess and aesthetic value. Against such biases, we should try to appreciate where possible the potential for diversity at Levels 1, 2, and 3 just as we do appreciate, or know we should, how different sports themselves exhibit beautiful variety at Level 4. Against mostly monolithic models of athletic technique and physique, we should appreciate how athletic prowess is often, if admittedly not always, multiply realizable across different sports as well as individual athletes, techniques, and physiques (ibid.: 213). Sometimes taking a critical perspective on optimization models in biomechanics may help reveal faults in presumed homogenization.[4] Valuing diversity hence becomes warranted not only from a biological or political point of view but from an epistemic and aesthetic point of view as well, whether in sport or life generally. We should note again, however, that this works against a will to simplicity, which I have argued is an aesthetic virtue only where it gets the relevant facts right. Trying to force everyone, in some ill-motivated procrustean way, into forms of movement they need not, best not, and cannot adopt has no more than a superficial and ultimately harmful appeal covering up an ugliness in the attempt. It is in this spirit, therefore, that I turn to aesthetic biases in sport that reflect wider concerns with matters of social justice.

Aesthetic injustice

Among the more obvious forms of aesthetic injustice in sport cultures are group biases, based on stereotypes, that tend to over- or underrate the aesthetic and other qualities of athletic movements and performances. Many take the form of prejudices. For example, though the hyperathletic bias inclines us to be too generous in assessing the prowess and performances of stereotypically lean and muscular athletic physiques, this bias manifests itself differently depending on the athlete's gender and expresses prejudice against athletic- and unathletic-looking women alike. There is a tendency to see leaner and more muscular physiques as not just more athletically capable – even where this doesn't apply, as in golf – but also as more masculine. But this tendency favors men in that the same physical appearances that *seem* most athletically capable coincide seamlessly with cultural expectations of masculinity. A man with an athletic-looking physique appears to be more of an athlete and more of a man besides: a double victory.

On the other hand, these norms also apply to female athletes. But here the double victory is impossible, because athletic-looking physiques only partly coincide with norms of femininity. Both are supposed to be lean but only one – the athlete's – is supposed to be muscular, and thus the stereotypically athletic physique unjustly both flatters men and insults women as masculine, even though the image itself as we have seen proves inaccurate, even as a benchmark of athletic prowess. Hence female athletes who look feminine are likely to have both their athleticism and its proper aesthetic properties marginalized in (dis)favor of overexposure for the wrong reasons: an oversexualized, underathleticized sense of an athlete's beauty or cachet (e.g., Anna Kournikova). On the other hand, those who fit the athletic stereotype thereby appear to violate feminine norms and are likely to find their athletic achievements diminished by a culture disappointed by what it registers, even subconsciously, as misplaced masculinity (e.g., Serena Williams or, indeed, many other dominant women in tennis history). The culture thus presents women a constructive dilemma in which the aesthetic appeal of their athleticism will be compromised by an appearance that either fits or fails to fit cultural expectations of femininity.

There may appear to be a way out in the form of sports where women have physiological advantages or that appear to be more compatible with feminine norms than masculine sports do.[5] Many of these are aesthetic sports in which athletes are judged on form and other aesthetic features and women's physiological characteristics are no hindrance and sometimes a distinct advantage: figure skating, diving, gymnastics, synchronized swimming, for some of the more intuitive cases.

Following Jane English's lead, 'Perhaps the most extreme example of a sport favoring women's natural skills is the balance beam. Here, small size, flexibility and low center of gravity combine to give women the kind of natural hegemony that men enjoy in football' (2003: 228).[6] However, it would be a mistake to posit feminine sports and aesthetic sports as coextensive. Various skiing events, including the long jump as well as aerials, moguls, and other freestyle events, are judged partly on aesthetic grounds and yet do not seem to compromise the heteronormative masculinity of male participants the way that other aesthetic sports appear to or cohere in the same way with norms of femininity. This likely owes to a sort of daredevil mentality associated with competing in these events. Even more striking perhaps are rodeo events judged on style points, which in no way seem to compromise riders' masculinity. Still, though, limiting ourselves to aesthetic sports seemingly consistent with feminine norms, what we end up with is not a way out of the dilemma but rather a *tri*lemma: one either compromises femininity for the sake of athleticism in masculine sports, has one's femininity overshadow the beauty of athleticism, or, by compromising neither, excels in a sport itself considered inferior for being feminine. This is especially ironic in the case of gymnastics, whose reach extends all the way back to antiquity yet which to the modern mind skews feminine (although admittedly, to some extent, so does antiquity itself). Even worse, gymnastics and other such seemingly feminine-friendly sports often pose greater health risks to women and girls than any sport or other activity reasonably should.

Not all such group biases are negative, however, as we may often be inclined to overrate the athletic achievements or style of members of groups that have disproportionately dominated in certain sports. Such trends often have geocultural and sometimes racial dimensions. Consider the prominence of black athletes from Ethiopia in marathon running, or from Jamaica in sprints, or from the United States in basketball. Some expectations of prowess in these cases will derive from positive biases, however problematic the stereotypes or their inductive bases. Likewise, we may be positively biased toward hockey players from Canada and Russia among other countries in northern climes, soccer players from Europe and South America, and so forth. Positive biases likewise loom over class expectations, from upper-class polo players to working-class boxers, or what have you. Much as the decathlon is usually taken to be the ultimate test of athletic prowess, the sport that holds perhaps the greatest aesthetic piquancy for me is the modern pentathlon, and I strongly suspect that this owes in no small part to its test of diverse skills that mark an unusual physical literacy and prowess among a certain military class.[7]

Positive biases are often counterbalanced, expectedly and problematically, by prejudices. We may wrongly expect better and more beautiful performances from black athletes on the track than in the natatorium. Athletes who flout such stereotypes likely find the beauty of their efforts underrated by some and overrated by others because of quite different attitudes toward the same stereotypes. Besides gender, race, nationality, and class, we should also mention other categories that can likewise split aesthetic response along social justice lines: sexual orientation, physical and intellectual disabilities, and intersex and trans status. The unfamiliarity of much Paralympic or Special Olympic competition tends to upset closed-minded sensibilities of people opposed to multiple realizability and diversity generally. As well, intersex and trans athletes present further difficulties to sport institutions as they are, upsetting not only dichotomized gender concepts but also dichotomized competitions. The consequent loss of elegance and (over)simplicity may spur complaints that are, if ultimately unjust, partly pragmatic, partly aesthetic.

In this way, group biases exhibit a kind of aesthetic–moral interaction different from that posited by Mumford and discussed in Chapter 5. The idea there was implicitly normative: where an athlete plays courageously, for instance, we *ought* at least sometimes to find the aesthetics of their performance enhanced. Here, however, we have the descriptive counterpart of the plausible normative principle. Moral and aesthetic injustices tend to coincide in sport – and elsewhere – in that aesthetic injustice is often predicated on social injustice and vice versa, marginalized groups tending to be denied their due in other ways as well as aesthetically and privileged groups often getting more than their fair share. Such biases, of course, whether negative or positive, should be minimized in aesthetic judgments of sport, as elsewhere. However, to the extent that an athlete's efforts violate rather than conforming to unjust social expectations, that will, all else being equal, require them to be more courageous, which against a prejudice that finds it ugly should rather be seen and celebrated as more beautiful. Rather than an offsetting bias, this would be a measure of aesthetic justice past due.

Space does not permit more than brief mention of how the media play into such aesthetic injustice by both reflecting and reinforcing the prejudices and biases on which it is based. It will be no surprise that traditional feminine norms, for instance, are deeply entrenched in the framing of sport in the contemporary media landscape.[8] The reasons for this are clear enough. Whatever the mandate of journalistic and other media outlets, the profit motive looms large, and profits are usually easier to accrue by catering to rather than challenging the biased and prejudicial tastes of one's target audience. However slowly progress is made on issues of social justice in the culture at large, sport subcultures almost invariably lag behind, moving at a virtually glacial pace. Even worse than more traditional media, though, are social media, where it is the most extreme views that reap the rewards of attention, with the substantial restraint and accountability of more traditional media left far behind. The unbridled social *regress* that lurks unashamedly in plain sight on the Internet makes it painfully clear that many kinds of justice we should like to see in the world, including the broadly symptomatic concern with aesthetic justice in sport, is in some ways much further away than many of us would find truly beautiful.

Notes

1 The Lady Byng Memorial trophy is awarded for the combination of sportsmanship and a high level of playing ability, thus representing in a broad sense the virtues of the game.
2 On epistemic injustice see for example Fricker (2007).
3 See Holt and Holt (2010: 212–14, 217), where we extrapolate, with appropriate qualifications, from golf to other sport subcultures.
4 On this point see Yeadon (2005: 136, 140). See also Holt and Holt (2010: 211–12).
5 On different ways of drawing the masculine/feminine sport distinction, see Postow (1988: 324).
6 The beam is exclusively a women's event, but perhaps it should not be. It would be instructive to introduce men's beam competitions. Note English's call for 'developing a variety of sports, in which a variety of physical types can be expected to excel' (2003: 228).
7 No doubt personal significance is involved here too, as I have some wherewithal in four of the five skill domains.
8 See for instance various articles by Weaving (e.g., 2010, 2012, 2013).

References

English, J. (2003) 'Sex Equality in Sports', in J. Boxill (ed.) *Sports Ethics: An Anthology*, Malden, MA: Blackwell, pp. 225–9.
Fricker, M. (2007) *Epistemic Injustice: Power and the Ethics of Knowing*, Oxford: Oxford University Press.
Holt, J. and Holt, L. E. (2010) 'The "Ideal" Swing, the "Ideal" Body: Myths of Optimization', in A. Wible (ed.) *Golf and Philosophy: Lessons from the Links*, Lexington: University Press of Kentucky, pp. 209–20.

Hume, D. (2002) 'Of the Standard of Taste', in T. E. Wartenberg (ed.) *The Nature of Art: An Anthology*, Orlando: Harcourt, pp. 39–47.

Postow, B. C. (1988) 'Women and Masculine Sports', in W. J. Morgan and K. V. Meier (eds.) *Philosophic Inquiry in Sport* (2nd Ed.), Champaign, IL: Human Kinetics, pp. 323–8.

Weaving, C. (2010) 'Unraveling the Ideological Concept of the Female Athlete: A Connection Between Sex and Sport', in P. Davis and C. Weaving (eds.) *Philosophical Perspectives on Gender and Sport*, London: Routledge, pp. 83–94.

Weaving, C. (2012) 'Smoke and Mirrors: A Feminist Critique of Women Olympians' Nude Reflections', *Sport, Ethics and Philosophy*, 6 (2): 232–50.

Weaving, C. (2013) 'Cage Fighting Like a Girl: Exploring Gender Constructions in the Ultimate Fighting Championship (UFC)', *Journal of the Philosophy of Sport*, 41 (1): 129–42.

Yeadon, M. R. (2005) 'What Are the Limitations of Experimental and Theoretical Approaches in Sports Biomechanics?', in M. McNamee (ed.) *Philosophy and the Sciences of Exercise, Health and Sport: Critical Perspectives on Research Methods*, New York: Routledge, pp. 133–43.

7 Aesthetic sports

In advocating a pluralist approach to sport aesthetics, I have had to rule out extreme subjectivism according to which any aesthetic response to sport is equally legitimate, that anything goes when it comes to not only a person's aesthetic preferences but her judgments as well. One part of my response to this problem, in the preceding chapter, was to elaborate how the presence of certain biases can undermine aesthetic judgment, the latter often inflicting some form of what I called aesthetic injustice. But this is only a partial solution to the problem, since lack of bias is necessary but not sufficient for good judgment. It remains possible that different unbiased judgments of sport may yield different aesthetic assessments in evaluating or comparing from an aesthetic point of view different performances, styles, or sports themselves. Sometimes, in the realm of preferences, for instance, we should expect such divergence, but not always. We often approach consensus about which sport movements are beautiful, and why. Nor is this a random matter. What we need is at least some explanation of how transpersonal aesthetic judgment is possible so that in many cases disagreements can be resolved as a matter of principle or practice.

Although such an explanation is desirable in the case of purposive sports, however, it is not necessary either for uncovering the basic nature of such activities – bracketing the aesthetics of game design – or making sense of discourse concerning them. The same is *not* true, however, for aesthetic sports, since here we expect judges more or less to concur on the aesthetic value of performances so that athletes get the score they deserve. Officials in purposive sports may make the wrong call sometimes, but the effect of such mistakes on competitive outcomes, at least most of the time, is comparatively minimal, whereas awarding style points properly in aesthetic sports is always of paramount importance. If we cannot articulate an objective basis for either aesthetic judgment or what in judged sports appears very much like aesthetic judgment, that will reveal an inherent flaw in aesthetic sport design. If we can articulate an objective basis for such judgment in sport, however, that will vindicate belief in the legitimacy of transpersonal aesthetic judgment in sport generally, as well as our sense that aesthetic sports are built on different but no less solid foundations than purposive sports. Some people unfairly consider aesthetic sports to be lesser or not even *real* sports at all, because in relying on aesthetic judgment they appear problematically subjective, to lack the same factual basis for judgment that we find in purposive sports. Thus, by vindicating transpersonal aesthetic judgment, we should be able to counteract a widespread and, I believe, implicitly aesthetic bias against aesthetic sports.

The purposive/aesthetic distinction

We have already encountered in earlier chapters the distinction between purposive and aesthetic sports. In Chapter 2 I argued that graceful movement is realized differently in these two types of sport: by the fluid integration of movements in purposive sports and by economy and efficiency of movements in aesthetic sports, since in the latter ideal forms are prescribed in advance. Then, in Chapter 4, I argued that purposive and aesthetic sports exhibit a degree of dependent and free beauty, respectively, since the former is defined in terms of a competitive purpose (e.g., scoring a goal), where the latter may be appreciated irrespective of competitive context (e.g., cliff diving). Aesthetic sports were characterized as those whose competitive outcomes are partly determined according to judged aesthetic criteria: athletes are awarded points for style, good form, aesthetic quality, or artistic impression. This is because, as Best puts it, 'an aesthetic sport is one in which the purpose cannot be specified independently of the manner of achieving it' (1978: 105). As for assessing such style of achievement, this falls to the expertise of impaneled judges. 'A purposive sport', by contrast, 'is one in which, within the rules or conventions, there is an indefinite variety of ways of achieving the end which at least largely defines the game' (ibid.: 104–5). So, whereas ice hockey qualifies as a purposive sport, ice dance qualifies as an aesthetic sport.

Where Best prefers the term 'aesthetic' to refer to such paradigms as diving, gymnastics, and figure skating, Kupfer opts for 'qualitative/formal' (1988), Suits 'performance' (1988), and Hurka 'judged' (2015). Whatever terms we adopt, these types are considered to be exhaustive in that every sport will be characterizable either as purposive, aesthetic, or some combination of the two. McFee gives an example of a blended case: 'the scoring in ski-jumping awards some marks for distance (purposive), and some for style (aesthetic). So ski-jumping is a straightforward mix of Best's two categories' (2004: 91). Similarly, Arnold speaks of what he calls *partially* aesthetic sports (2014: 184), and so both Arnold and McFee follow Best's drawing of the distinction, with purposive sports or elements being those in which the purpose *can* be specified independent of the manner of achieving it.

This characterization is questionable, however. First, in aesthetic sports there is usually a distinction between technical and stylistic elements, typically the remit of different judges using different criteria to determine separate elements then combined into total scores. This means that in a crucial sense we can distinguish between *what* an athlete does (how many somersaults, say) and *how* or how well she does it. Second, even if we agree with Best that in the gymnastics vault, 'the aim cannot be specified simply as "getting over the box", but only in terms of the manner of achievement required' (1978: 104), this has analogies in purposive sports and so on its own will not suffice to distinguish aesthetic sports.[1] Just as not every clearing of the box counts as a vault, not every goalward launching of a hockey puck counts as a shot, since kicking and throwing the puck are disallowed, as is batting the puck in the air above shoulder height with one's stick. In the same way, different types of shots (slap, snap, and wrist) are defined partly by how the shots are taken. As means/end separability is far less clearly distinctive in the two types of sport than Best suggests, it would be better to characterize aesthetic sports as those in which outcomes are partly determined by aesthetic judgment. This means ski-jumping should be classified not as a blended case but as an aesthetic sport *simpliciter*, though at this point the dispute may seem to be merely terminological. Still, if we insist that ski-jumping is a blended case because of the separability of purposive and aesthetic elements, this would also apply to many paradigm aesthetic sports (e.g., figure skating). On reflection, these would have to be recast as blended cases, a counterintuitive and better avoided revision.

The more interesting and rarer kinds of blended cases are those that may be purposive and aesthetic by turns. In some rodeo events, bull riding for instance, one must stay mounted for a designated time (eight seconds). If only one rider stays on the full time, that rider wins – a purposive outcome determiner. If, however, more than one rider makes it through, the winner is decided by style points – an aesthetic outcome determiner. In this way, such events are what might be called purposive/aesthetic sports, in that their outcomes are decided sometimes purposively, sometimes aesthetically. I have jointly explored in this vein the counterintuitive possibility that, of all sports, *boxing* constitutes a purposive/aesthetic sport (Yeomans and Holt 2015). Boxing certainly seems to be a purposive sport, for it seems, following Suits (2015: 51), a paradigm physical game (i.e., *not* a performance sport): 'an extremely effective way to achieve the prelusory goal in a boxing match – viz., the state of affairs consisting in your opponent being "down" for the count of[ ]ten – is to shoot him through the head, but this is obviously not a means for winning the match'.[2] In fact, however, boxing is only obviously purposive with wins by knockout or technical knockout. When this does not happen, the judges decide who wins in virtue of points scored. It might seem that points are purposive, too, tallied simply in virtue of the number of punches landed, but this is not entirely true: 'The scoring system of professional boxing allows judges to give boxers points if they feel as though the boxer had cleaner punches, higher aggression, better defense, and more control of the ring relative to their opponent' (Yeomans and Holt 2015: 91).[3] If judges may, and should, award more points in virtue of how *well* a boxer boxed (*quality* of punches, ring control, and so on), then the determination of scores and final decision is significantly qualitative, which appears to meet various criteria for aesthetic sports, including Best's, Kupfer's, and even Suits's. This means that in cases of wins by decision, boxing turns out to be an aesthetic sport, even if in counting points judges are not *explicitly* charged with awarding what we would tend to call style points. So boxing, like bull riding, is arguably a purposive/aesthetic sport. Yet whether this point merely reinforces the criticism of Best's criterion (inter alia) for distinguishing purposive from aesthetic sports or, granting it, opens surprising implications for classifying different types of sports, I leave to the reader's judgment.

Game status

Part of the reason Suits's theory of games holds a place of unique significance in the philosophy of sport is that sports seem to be certain kinds of physical games. We should recall from Chapter 4 that in Suits's view games involve both prelusory goals, specifiable independently of the rules, and constitutive rules, which define a game, constrain game activity, and are accepted by players because they make the activity possible. Despite the explanatory power of Suits's account vis-à-vis sport, acknowledged in earlier work, on his more mature view (1988) he abandons the notion that all sports are games. Suits's specific argument is that performance (i.e., aesthetic) sports are sufficiently unlike game (i.e., purposive) sports to fail to qualify as genuine games. Unlike true game sports, Suits believes, performance sports are judged, not refereed; they are rehearsed, not practiced;

they require artistry, not efficacy; the skills are natural, not artificial; their governance is by formal ideals, not constitutive rules (e.g., the offside rule in some purposive sports) (1988: 17, 19). In aesthetic sports like diving, there is nothing that approximates a referee stopping play because of a rule infraction. Of a piece with this is the comparative difficulty, as Suits sees it, in specifying prelusory goals for such sports (1989: 1). Whereas the prelusory goal of a footrace is to cross a certain line (lusorily the finish line) first, there seems no comparably clear counterpart in diving and similar sports.

With a certain air of paradox, perhaps, Klaus Meier defends Suits against himself, that is, Suits's early view that all sports are games from the later view that performance/aesthetic sports are not games. First, Meier claims, although performance sports do lack rules such as the offside rule – imagine the absurdity of an official trying to whistle down a diver mid-dive – that is not a problem for the game status of performance sports, for these rules turn out to be not constitutive but *regulative*, that is, governing how activity is to proceed rather than defining what it is (1988: 20). When a player goes offside, as often happens in sports with an offside rule (e.g., American football, hockey, soccer, rugby), on Suits's formalist view it is not that the player has made an illegal move but rather that he has failed to play at all, a less plausible interpretation. Further, Meier notes that if we focus on Suits's compressed definition of game-playing – the voluntary attempt to overcome unnecessary obstacles – the gamelike qualities of aesthetic sports come to the fore. For example, the height of a diving board is an unnecessary obstacle in that it would be easier to jump into the water from poolside, or to perform a certain number of rotations, or what have you, from a greater height (ibid.: 22). Moreover, Meier observes (ibid.: 19), Suits himself embraces a kind of rule minimalism about game status; in his Rien-à-faire thought experiment, for instance, in a supposedly no-rules fight to the death, so long as there is *some* artificial restriction in place, such as an agreed-to start time, the contest will qualify as a game (2005: 74–5). As performance sport contests have many more rules besides (e.g., start times, order, intervals), some of them constitutive (e.g., concerning apparatus), they have an even better claim to game status than Suits's Rien-à-faire scenario. In essence, Meier has done intellectual aikido by marshalling the strength of Suits's own argument against him.

Elsewhere, however, Suits maintains (1989: 1) that the problem with counting sports like diving as games is less the apparent lack of constitutive rules and more the difficulty of picking out prelusory goals. Taking diving as his paradigm, Suits argues that none of the best candidates for the prelusory goal – total submersion in water, vertical entry, or the entire dive itself – can be justified (ibid.: 7). Where Kretchmar (1989: 36) argues that we can make sense of submersion as the prelusory goal of diving, Hurka (2015: 317) proposes rather that the prelusory goal is to dive beautifully (though Suits might challenge this as not counting as a *specific* state of affairs); thus Kretchmar locates the aesthetics of diving in the rules, where Hurka locates it in the objective of the activity itself. I suggest that both Kretchmar and Hurka get something right here. If one is to end up in water, one can make a game of it by making it harder, by diving, rather than sliding in at poolside, say. By doing so, the inevitable end state of being in the water becomes *prelusified*, just as in Suits's Rien-à-faire scenario the inevitable state of being dead (any contestant will die eventually) is prelusified by games of mortal combat. Likewise, one can aim to dive beautifully, or *well*, outside any competitive context. But whereas both proposals may capture what it means to make getting into the water a game by diving to do so, neither appears suitable to characterize core sport cases (i.e., diving *competitions*), because these are not won simply by diving or diving beautifully. Here the prelusory goal is to dive *best*, not just beautifully but the most beautifully, just as (to use a Suitsian example) the prelusory goal of a footrace is to cross a certain line *first*. What 'best' or 'most beautifully' means here is a combination of technical difficulty and formal precision, with aesthetic appeal factored in. Just as footrace rules designate where the finish line is, so too do diving rules determine what kinds and qualities of dive are best.

Perhaps, though, the prelusory goal of a footrace is to run the *fastest* instead of crossing a certain line first.[4] If we acknowledge some degree of indeterminacy in specifying prelusory goals in Suits's paradigm cases, perhaps the moral is that on a Suitsian account of games what we need is one *or more* prelusory specifications that are plausible. Alternatively, we may note comparable difficulties in specifying prelusory goals for games in virtual environments, including chess and videogames.[5] How, for instance, is the lusory goal of chess, checkmate, describable in prelusory terms, that is, without appealing to the rules? Likewise, if we consider videogames, 'In a virtual race game, for instance, there is no game-independently drawable line a first crossing of which can constitute the prelusory goal, just as there is no actual space in which one is able to draw the line' (Holt 2016: 10). Perhaps we need to jettison the idea that games require prelusory goals, or perhaps we can adopt a deflationary strategy that takes any lusory goal (e.g., having the highest score) and reduces it to some nominal description (e.g., having the highest number beside one's name, standing atop the podium, holding the yellowish medal, and so on) (ibid.: 11). Among all such possibilities, it is more plausible to retain rather than abandon the game status of diving and other aesthetic sports.

The subjectivity problem

There is often a superficial suspicion of aesthetic judgment in general, and especially in domains such as the artworld and the sportworld, where aesthetics can be highly prized. Such a suspicion paradoxically touches on perhaps the deepest philosophical question concerning aesthetic sports and aesthetic judgment generally: the subjectivity problem. One often may get the sense that art critics, whose opinions often diverge widely, pontificate from the pulpit of their own arbitrary if educated preferences. Among officials in aesthetic sports, though, there tends to be much greater convergence of opinion, for here judgments are more significantly constrained by facts (not that art criticism is somehow *un*constrained by facts). There are facts of the matter about whether, for instance, an athlete maintains or breaks form. Neither is awarding points for degree of difficulty, deductions for certain imperfections, or style points generally arbitrary. Rules and procedures tend to funnel expert judgments into approximate consensus most of the time. It will be rare, for instance, that judges' scores will vary problematically *widely*, even if they cluster around a mean rather than being identical across the board. Likewise, especially where scoring design has been conscientiously modified, there are methods in place for minimizing effects of potentially biased outliers (e.g., by discounting the highest and lowest marks). In my view, part of the suspicion of aesthetic sports and art criticism, chiefly outsiders' suspicion of the cognoscenti, comes from the fact that the expertise required for discrimination and judgment often eludes ordinary perception and understanding. Watching a purposive sport in real time or in slow-motion replay, most of us will be able to make the right call, but this is frequently not so with aesthetic sports, even where expert commentary helps to guide our observations. Although watching slow-motion replays of aesthetic sport performances makes it easier for us to see some of what expert judges see in real time (or with the aid of video replay), most of us are unable to tell just by looking which among comparable performances is best. In the same way, critics often understand more than the casual artgoing public about works of art. Expert judgment, whether about aesthetic sports or artworks, often discerns – to adapt a phrase from Danto – what the common eye cannot descry.

A lot depends on expert judgment here. But what is it that endows these experts with the ability to make transpersonal judgments about matters of taste? One classic account of how such judgments are possible is developed in David Hume's 'Of the Standard of Taste', first published in 1757, in which he characteristically appeals to the uniformity of human nature: 'the principles of taste be universal, and nearly, if not entirely the same in all men; yet few are qualified to give judgment on any work of art, or establish their own sentiment as the standard of beauty' (2002: 44). The reason for such rarity of expertise, as Hume sees it, is that 'organs of internal sensation are seldom so perfect as to allow the general principles their full play' (ibid.). This is caused by various factors that often undermine individual tastes as representative, and this accounts for the proliferation of disagreements in matters of taste. Some would-be judges are unable to make the appropriate fine-grained discriminations of aesthetically relevant properties, others to respond to such discriminations properly. Others still are unpracticed or have too limited experience with a suitably wide range of instances. Finally, occurrent bias or prejudice may undermine judgments of taste otherwise fine grained, responsive, practiced, and widely experienced. So, for Hume, true expertise exhibits the following properties: 'Strong sense, united to delicate sentiment, improved by practice, perfected by comparison, and cleared of all prejudice' (ibid.).[6] The difficulty will be trying to figure out who, if anyone, meets these criteria. It is one thing to evince that someone has failed to clear one or more of these hurdles, but absent such evidence one has no more than a tenuous claim to expert status.

In the case of genuine disagreement about taste, it seems at least one of the verdicts must be erroneous. Not all apparent disagreements are genuine disagreements, however. Hume relates an anecdote from *Don Quixote* in which two wine experts are derided for finding different faults with an otherwise good wine: one notes a slight metallic taste, the other a slight leather taste; but when the keg is drained they find an iron key on a leather strap (ibid.: 43). The disagreement was merely apparent, both oenophiles correctly grasping different parts of the elephant. This parallels McFee's discussion of ambiguous figures as analogous to cases in aesthetic sports (2004: 94–6). Just as ambiguous figures (like the Necker cube, although that is not McFee's example) support different independently supportable interpretations, so too can borderline or ambiguous cases in aesthetic sports – or sport generally – revert to the judgment call of officials. Indeed, for McFee judgment calls in aesthetic sports are on a par with and no more problematic than judgment calls in purposive sports like football or baseball, although in the former the role of officials, again, is more crucial (ibid.: 97).

As expert judgment in aesthetic sports often eludes ordinary sportgoers, cases of scandal are particularly vexing. Case in point: the pairs figure skating at the 2002 Salt Lake City Winter Olympics, in which the Russians Elena Berezhnaya and Anton Sikharulidze were scored above the Canadian pair, Jamie Salé and David Pelletier, even though the former had noteworthy flaws in their routine, which won gold, where the latter, with a comparably difficult routine, had none, winning silver. When officials concluded that this result was mistaken and that evidence pointed to bribery and fixed judging, they split the difference between respecting and correcting the call, promoting the Canadians' silver to gold without demoting the Russians to silver. Apropos, some philosophers of sport fail to agree on a description of the case. Nicholas Dixon: 'the Canadians' [routine] was faultless. Unless the Russians' routine was more technically challenging or clearly superior in artistic merit – which was patently not the case, in the opinion of nearly all observers – the Canadians should have won' (2003: 103). But as Graham McFee recounts, 'this is certainly not my recollection – the Canadian skaters certainly pleased the (largely partisan) crowd, but was their skating superior to the trained eyes of the judges? It may be hard to tell' (2004: 98).[7] True, we cannot be absolutely certain about how the judges saw things, but as *I* remember the scandal, Dixon's take is better justified where McFee's is unduly skeptical. It was not just the crowd but a slew of expert commentators in the figure skating world who concluded that something had gone wrong. But could this just be my Canadian partisanship showing through?

When we cannot decide between competing divergent expert opinions, that is, where we cannot ascertain that one fails to meet Hume's criteria, we should suspend judgment or perhaps conclude that on some questions of taste human nature remains equivocal or silent. For instance, we might be reasonably confident that Jane Austen is a great writer and that Charles Dickens is too, but we should be far less so in judging or resolving expert disputes about which if either is the better writer, whether overall or in comparing works from each. Yet the latter is precisely the sort of difficulty apparently faced by judges in aesthetic sports. Now there may be no fact of the matter about whether *Pride and Prejudice* ranks as aesthetically better or worse than or equivalent to *A Tale of Two Cities*, but by analogy that is exactly the sort of determination we expect to be made by aesthetic sport judges. But there are at least two crucial differences between cases of aesthetic judgment in the artworld and in the sportworld. First, the comparison of Austen's and Dickens's work, in the realm of art, is of comparably little importance, being nowhere close to the point of art or appreciating quality literature. By contrast, however, determining whether Berezhnaya and Sikharulidze or Salé and Pelletier had the better pairs performance lies at the very heart of figure skating competitions. And even if human nature were silent – which again, it isn't – about which performance was better from an aesthetic point of view, the judging procedures of figure skating, the rules and logic of the game, are not.[8] Judging in aesthetic sports has a forced conventionality, a certain justified artificiality, to assist judges in rigorously and precisely adjudicating close and ambiguous cases that would elude the finest-grained, unaided expertise. For aesthetic sports this is not a weakness but a strength. In the interest of aesthetic and athletic justice, the right practice can extend the most refined taste beyond its own natural limits. Thus aesthetic judgment, though grounded in the artworld, is better grounded in the sportworld. It has to be.

Notes

1 Compare with Roberts's critique (1986) of Best's separation of sport and art partly because the former apparently does, whereas the latter does not, allow a distinction between ends and means. I leave the art-as-sport question for Chapter 9.
2 On Suits's mature view (1988), performance (aesthetic) sports fail to count as games. I address this issue later.
3 Yeomans and Holt (ibid.) cite Thomson (2012) here.
4 On this point see Berman (2013: 164).
5 See Schneider and Butcher (1997: 39) and Holt (2016: 10), respectively.
6 See Levinson (2006: 368, 382) for an updated ideal critic account inspired by Hume's original theory.
7 McFee is actually responding here not to Dixon but to a newspaper article expressing virtually the same point, so he might as well be answering Dixon.
8 On this point compare Kuntz's claim (1974: 11) that judges in aesthetic sports need to be more conservative than judges in the arts.

References

Arnold, P. J. (2014) 'Sport, the Aesthetic and Art: Further Thoughts', in J. Holt (ed.) *Philosophy of Sport: Core Readings*, Peterborough: Broadview Press, pp. 179–98.

Berman, M. N. (2013) 'Sprints, Sports, and Suits', *Journal of the Philosophy of Sport*, *40* (1): 63–76.

Best, D. (1978) *Philosophy and Human Movement*, London: George Allen & Unwin.

Dixon, N. (2003) 'Canadian Figure Skaters, French Judges, and Realism in Sport', *Journal of the Philosophy of Sport*, *30* (2): 103–16.

Holt, J. (2016) 'Virtual Domains for Sports and Games', *Sport, Ethics and Philosophy*, *10* (1): 5–13.

Hume, D. (2002) 'Of the Standard of Taste', in T. E. Wartenberg (ed.) *The Nature of Art: An Anthology*, Orlando: Harcourt, pp. 39–47.

Hurka, T. (2015) 'On Judged Sports', *Journal of the Philosophy of Sport*, *42* (3): 317–25.

Kretchmar, R. S. (1989) 'On Beautiful Games', *Journal of the Philosophy of Sport, 16*: 34–43.

Kuntz, P. G. (1974) 'Aesthetics Applies to Sports as Well as to the Arts', *Journal of the Philosophy of Sport, 1*: 7–35.

Kupfer, J. H. (1988) 'Sport – The Body Electric', in W. J. Morgan and K. V. Meier (eds.) *Philosophic Inquiry in Sport* (2nd Ed.), Champaign, IL: Human Kinetics, pp. 390–406.

Levinson, J. (2006) *Contemplating Art*, Oxford: Clarendon Press.

McFee, G. (2004) *Sport, Rules and Values: Philosophical Investigations into the Nature of Sport*, New York: Routledge.

Meier, K. V. (1988) 'Triad Trickery: Playing with Sports and Games', *Journal of the Philosophy of Sport, 15*: 11–30.

Roberts, T. J. (1986) 'Sport, Art, and Particularity: The Best Equivocation', *Journal of the Philosophy of Sport, 13*: 49–63.

Schneider, A. J. and Butcher, R. B. (1997) 'Pre-lusory Goals for Games: A Gambit Declined', *Journal of the Philosophy of Sport, 24*: 38–46.

Suits, B. (1988) 'Tricky Triad: Games, Play, and Sport', in W. J. Morgan and K. V. Meier (eds.) *Philosophic Inquiry in Sport* (2nd Ed.), Champaign, IL: Human Kinetics, pp. 16–22.

Suits, B. (1989) 'The Trick of the Disappearing Goal', *Journal of the Philosophy of Sport, 16*: 1–12.

Suits, B. (2005) *The Grasshopper: Games, Life and Utopia* (2nd Ed.), Peterborough: Broadview.

Thomson, E. (2012) 'A Performance Analysis of Scoring in Professional Boxing: Can It Help?', *The Sport and Exercise Scientist, 33*: 12–3.

Yeomans, M. and Holt, J. (2015) 'Purposive/Aesthetic Sport: A Note on Boxing', *Fair Play, 3* (2): 87–95.

8   Sport in art

Back when the philosophy of sport was in its infancy (the 1970s!), a respectable portion of sport aesthetics was concerned with representations of sport in artistic media. In an early anthology of sport aesthetics, for instance, some 20 percent of the content engages directly with depictions of sport in visual and verbal media.[1] Likewise, Benjamin Lowe is not alone in seeing artworks with athletes as subjects to indicate and inform our aesthetic interest in sport and its artlike appeal and character: 'R. Tait McKenzie has brought a fine sense of movement to his athletic studies cast in bronze. . . . [T]he aesthetic qualities of these art works . . . provide intrinsic clues to our grasp of the elusive nature of beauty in sport' (1976, quoted in Best 1978: 122). Since that incipient time the fortunes of sport aesthetics have ebbed and flowed, yet there has been in my view precious little attention paid to questions about sport in art, even as sport aesthetics broadly seems to be on the rise toward a welcome renaissance. There have been sporadic exceptions to this trend, including occasional work on sport in literature (e.g., Wilberding 2017), sport film (e.g., de Melo 2012), as well as the historical curiosity of Olympic art competitions (e.g., Edgar 2012). Some of my own work draws heavily on the philosophical analysis of sport films.[2] Despite these efforts, however, the dearth is far more noticeable than the exceptions, and the latter mostly seem but tangentially related to theories of art and representation. This is a pity, for I believe, and hope to show in this chapter, that important philosophical insight may be gained from considering issues arising from artistic representations of sport.

The reason for this relative neglect, I suspect, is twofold. First, in what is surely the most important single text in the history of sport aesthetics, David Best's 'The Aesthetics of Sport', he offers strong arguments for the principled difference between sport and art (which I will address in the next chapter), including the distinction between sport *as* art and sport as represented *in* art (1978: 122). Second, there is a suspicion among many researchers in sport studies that artworks about sport might get the feelings right but, for all their virtues, get the facts wrong; if you *really* want to know boxing, say, better to watch actual fights than the *Rocky* films. Fair enough. Either reason would seem to suffice for questioning the potential value of subjecting sportistic artworks to philosophical analysis.[3] Even so, such analysis promises at least to uncover some of the ways we conceptualize, rightly or wrongly, the aesthetic and other aspects of sport. As well, sportistic artworks can provide raw material for thought experiments, giving purchase we would otherwise lack on theoretical speculation. Taking this as my cue, I will explore in turn depictions of sport in both static (e.g., sculpture) and dynamic (e.g., film) artforms, followed by a discussion of what I call the paradox of sport fiction.

Frozen movement

I begin with static depictions of sport in media like sculpture, painting, and photography. Where we encounter athletic movements and performances as extended in time, as unfolding processes, static artforms usually present only a single time-slice, a frozen instant of that process. However much such images may suggest movement, they freeze it (hence the term 'still').[4] Just as we can appreciate anatomy on its own (Level 1), in isolation from if suggestive of physiological function (Level 2), so does static sportistic artwork present a frozen structured moment divorced from but still part of the dynamic athletic event. Where we use language to describe some sporting event, we abstract from its particularities to describe it in terms that are necessarily more general. (That is what language does, and why a picture is worth rather more than a thousand words.) In visual artworks that freeze a single moment, however, we move in the opposite direction, as if singling out a single frame in a limitless film of indefinitely many frames. These are not then abstractions from the wholes that contain them, but the very opposite, which I propose we call *ad*stractions.[5] Static works of sportistic art *adstract* a frozen moment from the dynamic process, just as we can abstract from the moment to a linguistic description or visually to the entire event (though from either a verbal description or single visual image we could not predict or retrodict with accuracy what exactly the scene or its earlier and later stages would look like). Part of what we often find compelling about such works is that the artist has whittled down athleticism to its smallest visual part, an observational atom, as it were, that paradoxically freezes something essentially dynamic and, like all photography, makes permanent the ephemeral.

At the mention of sport sculpture, a mental image of one work in particular should spring to mind: Myron's *Discobolus* (discus thrower)

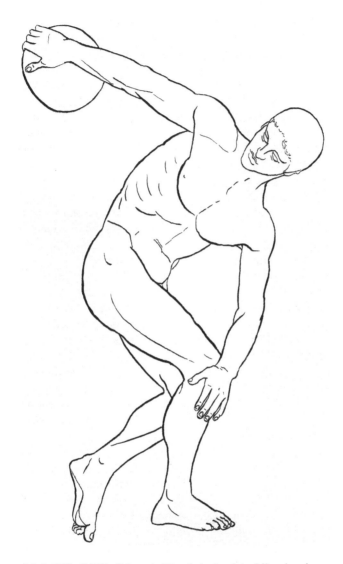

Figure 8.1 J. Wills (2019), 'Myron's *Discobolus*', original line drawing

(Figure 8.1). We do not actually have the original sculpture, which we know from notable Roman copies and photographs thereof. The *Discobolus* dates from around 450 BCE, and although there are many rival sculptural works that might have achieved such status instead, it stands alone in many ways as a paradigm work of art. It depicts a discus thrower at the apex of the preparatory loading phase, frozen at the moment he is about to explode into the ballistic throwing phase. The thrower's fine-tuned, conditioned physique, its lean, well-defined musculature, is on full display, though usually shown at an angle from which the right leg obscures the figure's genitalia. More important than the sculpture's inspired, highly skillful rendering of the figure and its perceptually available properties, however, is the cultural significance the work has acquired over the centuries, indeed millennia. As representing a single moment in the skillful movement of a niche if long-standing sport, the *Discobolus* has become an icon emblematic of sport itself – and more. As an emblem of sport itself, it is the paradigm work of sport sculpture, indeed, the paradigm work of sportistic art in general, one of the paradigmatic works of art period – and more. It functions as a symbol of human striving and achievement – of humanity itself. No other sport sculpture has become so universal, so deservedly clichéd, though the better any sport sculpture is, the more it tends to resonate with strains of such significance.

As with sport sculpture, there appears to be a tendency in sport painting and photography for the particular personalities of even famous people, recognizably depicted, to be utterly lost in a scene's symbolic significance. Consider Lowe's (1977: 134) description of an iconic image of Wilma Rudolph (ibid.: 159) winning gold in the 100 meters at the 1960 Rome Olympics: 'a fine sense of speed is conveyed . . . a strong notion of power . . . the obvious lightness and fleetness . . . the tilt of Wilma's head and her apparent "smile" adequately express what we understand by "the joy of effort"'. Even though the athlete's name is mentioned (yet why 'Wilma', not 'Rudolph'?), the momentous significance overwhelms it: Rudolph as type, as symbol, not Rudolph as person. This interpretative tendency is rather more pronounced in static works that convey an illusion of motion by multiplying images, as in Duchamp's painting *Nude Descending a Staircase, No. 2* or stroboscopic photographs of athletic movements where different time-slices are combined into a single flowing image. One important qualification, though: the depersonalizing tendency toward type applies to *in*-action images, where the movement is in process, rather than *re*action images, where the movement has ceased and the agent is responding to the result. If we consider iconic reaction shots in sport photography, where the athletic movement has ceased, the personality of the athlete seems unobscured by more general significance. Consider the famous photograph of Muhammad Ali standing over Sonny Liston after knocking him down (Neil Leifer) and that of Bobby Orr's celebratory layout after scoring a Stanley Cup–winning overtime goal (Ray

Lussie). Why in-action shots should obscure the very personalities that reaction shots express is a matter for further discussion, although part of the answer is that, whereas superlative actions are beyond most of us most of the time, emotional reactions by contrast are well within our reach.

These remarks imply a potential problem with attempts to create athletic portraits by depicting athletes in action, although the same does not hold in cases where an athlete poses. For Cynthia Freeland, for instance, a portrait requires three severally necessary and jointly sufficient conditions: the subject must be physically recognizable, possess an inner psychological life, and present a self in the form of posing (2010: 5, 17). Since in-action depictions of athletes are often not posed (although one can pose by mimicking an in-action posture, as with the common trope of aping the *Discobolus*), they cannot, on Freeland's account, qualify as portraits. Other theories of portraiture are more inclusive, however. For Paolo Spinicci, for instance, portraits are images subject to certain uses: 'What turns a picture into a portrait of x is the customary use we make of that picture as an image which is just about x and represents x in a particular way' (2009: 43). In Spinicci's view, then, an in-action depiction of an athlete may count as portrait if it is about that particular person represented in a particular way. Thus, the famous silhouette of Michael Jordan would not count as a portrait on Freeland's account but would on Spinicci's.

Perhaps surprisingly, according to these theories it is not only works of fine art that may count as portraits. As I argue elsewhere (forthcoming), sport cards (i.e., collectible trading cards of athletes) qualify as portraits on Freeland's view where they include posed photographs of the athletes in question. Though some sport cards use in-action rather than posed photos and are consequently excluded from the portrait class on Freeland's view, Spinicci's view would include them alongside the Jordan silhouette.[6] To characterize sport card portraiture correctly, we should acknowledge first that portraits may be done not just in visual media but in verbal media as well. Compare Whistler's *Portrait of the Artist's Mother* with Joyce's *Portrait of the Artist as a Young Man*. Indeed, sport card portraiture involves not only visual elements (usually a player photo) but also verbal elements (e.g., player metrics and statistics on the back). Because sport card portraits involve both visual and verbal elements, we can explain how error cards, which *mis*represent the athlete in some way, nonetheless count as portraits. They get some of the representations wrong (e.g., misspelled name), but even in those cases where a photograph of the wrong athlete is used, sufficient verbal elements remain to secure the subject's identity and record of achievement. The 1987 Donruss Opening Day #163 Barry Bonds rookie card counts as a Bonds card (and portrait) even though the photograph is not of Bonds himself but rather of his teammate Johnny Ray.[7] As sport cards illustrate, then, portraiture extends beyond the class of fine art to include examples of popular or mass art or perhaps further: beyond the reach of art itself.

Sports on film

Shifting our attention to dynamic representations of sport, consider broadcasts and recordings of actual sport performances, which we certainly would not count as works of art in anything like a normal sense of the term. Watching television broadcasts or content streamed on the Internet has become the dominant way of enjoying elite sports events. I concluded Chapter 6 by considering how the media reflect and reinforce aesthetically relevant biases; as a counterpoint here, though, I emphasize that, notwithstanding their distortive potential, the media also obviously provide an important avenue of access to sports events that to most of us most of the time would be virtually unavailable. To claim to have seen the big game – on television – raises no skeptic's hackles just because one failed to attend the event in person.[8] In several ways, in fact, watching broadcasts of sporting events provides a distinct epistemic advantage over live attendance (though one misses the full aura of the spectacle by not being swept up in the crowd). Because recordings allow for (re)play, often in slow motion and from multiple angles, no wonder that the use of video review by officials, including video assistant referees (VAR) in soccer, is becoming an increasingly key adjunct, especially in crucial situations, to help officials make the right call. As such technology continues to improve, it will appear more oddly arcane for officials to deny themselves judgment aids that broadcasters and fans have long enjoyed.

Techniques such as replay and slow motion are not simply advantages from an epistemic point of view either. They are also advantageous from an aesthetic point of view. In other words, watching a recording of a sporting movement in slow motion, or several times, or from different angles enhances our appreciation not merely of what the action *is*, what it achieves functionally, but also of its beauty, of what it achieves aesthetically. The reason for this, according to Best, is twofold: on one hand, 'we have more time to appreciate the manner of performance'; on the other, 'our attention is directed more to the character of the action than to its result. We can see whether and how every detail of every movement in the action as a whole contributes to making it' (1978: 108). Best's point here is further reflected in the use of such techniques in highlight reels, whose selection of clips and editing are guided by predominantly aesthetic considerations. Although in real time we often cannot anticipate much less fully absorb the full aesthetic power of the pretty play, we usually can to a far greater extent when watching (in *reel* time, as it were) the aesthetic concentrate that is the sport highlight reel. (There are limits, however. If the beauty of a sport performance emerges over the entire course of a game, this is obviously something the highlight reel cannot show.) The aesthetic appeal of the blooper reel, by contrast, is the comedic counterpart to our breathless wonder at the highlight reel. Despite the apotheosizing effect of the rewards they reap, not least our devout admiration, great athletes are, after all, only human.

When we consider the sport film as a distinct cinematic genre, however, other issues are foregrounded. For one thing, the genre comprises three broad types, each depending on a unique principal aim, which may be further subdivided: films that respectively document, dramatize, or fictionalize sport. The subgenre aiming to record athletic events and related cultural phenomena is naturally the sport documentary. Alongside more (sub)generic examples (e.g., *Olympia*, *Hoop Dreams*), we should note more recent experiments such as Gordon and Parreno's *Zidane: A 21st Century Portrait* (2006), which follows the midfielder Zinédine Zidane throughout an entire match, often in tight zoom (Real Madrid versus Villareal, 23 April 2005).[9] Sport dramatizations include biopics (e.g., *The Pride of the Yankees*), team stories (e.g., *Miracle*), and reenactments of historic sport events (e.g., *Battle of the Sexes*). Fictional sport film variations include (melo)drama (e.g., *The Loneliness of the Long Distance Runner*, *He Got Game*), comedy (e.g., *Slap Shot*, *A League of Their Own*), and fable (e.g., *The Natural*, *Field of Dreams*).[10] It takes little reflection to grasp that the sport film genre provides rather a broad variety of art and entertainment.

These sport film categories are not absolutely rigid. Often films will straddle or blur such distinctions and their corresponding artistic traditions alike. In the *Rocky* series, for instance, we find a blend of drama and melodrama, of realism and romanticism, a kind of gritty realism about life mixed with a rather unrealistic and idealistic romanticism about sport in general and boxing in particular.[11] In some cases, a sport film may also belong to another genre and realize a hybrid between the two. *The Set-Up*, for instance, a boxing movie starring Robert Ryan, counts as both a sport film and film noir. That Ryan had respectable collegiate boxing experience and on screen looks to be in fighting trim both underscore the realism connecting the two genres.[12] Indeed, the domain of the realistic boxing picture and that of film noir are one and the same, an intersection of mean streets in the same dark city.

A working definition of the sport film genre, then, might be the following: a sport film is one that highlights, by subject, sequence, or setting, at least one significant element of sport: an individual, team, event, subculture, or the activity itself.

For movies that are not primarily about sport yet include sport sequences or occur in sport settings, inclusion in the sport film genre will depend on whether these are of major or minor significance to the film. Using Sylvester Stallone films to illustrate, *Lock Up*, which contains a prison yard pickup football game, is not a real sport film, whereas *Victory*, a war film about POWs attempting to escape during an exhibition soccer game in the third act, does. However much our realist sensibilities may be irked by the idealism (or magic realism) of the cinematic fable or the oversimplified exaggerations of the melodrama, such unrealistic touches lend themselves to more effective symbolic representation of what sport ought to be. As I argue elsewhere (2017: 65–6), the artificially enhanced physique of a Sylvester Stallone plays into the peak shift effect – our tendency to respond more intensely to exaggerated stimuli – making him in *Rocky IV*, somewhat ironically, a more effective symbol of natural sport than anyone with a naturally built physique could have been.[13]

The paradox of sport fiction

The fact that many people care about sports at all much less deeply can seem from the outside a curious phenomenon. Getting deeply involved in events that, on some level, do not really matter strikes an odd note, as it does even among sport aficionados when they take a metaphorical step back from their personal investment and realize that, in contrast to the world's serious goings-on, their involvement in any given sport, or sport at all, has about it an air of arbitrary frivolity. In a way this is similar to the apparent peculiarity, again from the outside, of responding emotionally to fictional narratives, whether literary or cinematic.[14] From the inside, when one is caught up in sport or fiction, the personal investment, duly rewarded, seems perfectly reasonable. But there is nonetheless something puzzling, even paradoxical, about these investments, all the more so when they are compounded in caring about sport fiction. If our concern with the 'mere fun and games' of sport is puzzling and our emotional response to the 'mere stories' of fiction paradoxical, how much more puzzling a paradox is it to care about sport fiction? If sport doesn't really matter, and fiction doesn't either, how in the world could sport fiction possibly matter?

As this is what I call the paradox of sport fiction, it will behoove me to be explicate both the paradox of fiction, as it is commonly known, and the puzzle of sport, as Stear dubs it (2017: 275). The paradox of fiction is generated by three axiomatic but inconsistent propositions. Here is the formulation offered by Peter Lamarque:

(1) Readers or audiences often experience emotions such as fear, pity, desire, and admiration toward objects they know to be fictional, e.g., fictional characters.
(2) A necessary condition for experiencing emotions such as fear, pity, desire, etc., is that those experiencing them believe the objects of the emotions to exist.
(3) Readers or audiences who know that the objects are fictional do not believe that these objects exist.

(2003: 368)

It follows that either our emotional engagement in fictional narratives is irrational or that at least one of these propositions is false. Relatedly, Stear (2017: 275) describes the puzzle of sport as a kind of incongruity between fans' emotional reactions and reflective judgments: 'The outcomes of sports and competitive games excite intense emotions in many people, even when those same people acknowledge that those outcomes are of trifling importance'. We can follow Lamarque's rendering of the paradox of fiction in transposing mutatis mutandis Stear's puzzle of sport into a genuine paradox of sport, generated by the following three incompatible propositions:

1   Observers often experience emotions such as fear, pity, desire, and admiration toward objects they know to be matters of sport, e.g., game outcomes.
2   A necessary condition for experiencing emotions such as fear, pity, desire, etc., is that those experiencing them believe the objects of the emotions to matter.
3   Observers who know that the objects are sport matters do not believe that these objects really matter.

So either our emotional engagement with sport is irrational or one of these propositions is false. Even if emotional investment in sport is not paradoxical in this way, the paradox of sport fiction would remain in that, even if we can make sense of what doesn't really matter mattering, because it would matter if it *were* real, that by itself will not explain how what doesn't really matter *about* what doesn't really matter matters in the least. (Perhaps my project here is the ultimate curiosity: what doesn't really matter [i.e., philosophy] about what doesn't really matter [i.e., fiction] about what doesn't really matter [i.e., sport].)

The conclusion would seem to be either that our engagements in fiction, sport, and sport fiction are irrational or that we can identify one or more propositions in both paradox-generating sets that are false or otherwise limited. Vis-à-vis the paradox of fiction, I argue elsewhere (2008: 141) that we might feel genuine lower emotions like fear toward fictional objects, because lower emotions do not imply belief that the objects exist, since from an evolutionary point of view that would be disadvantageous, whereas fiction does not cause us to feel real higher emotions such as admiration, which do have such existential import, but merely make-believe or ersatz versions of such emotions. In terms of sport fiction, I really fear Drago, but I do not really admire Rocky – that is, I may feel real fear when I see Drago on screen, but I only quasi-admire Rocky, since I know that he does not really exist.[15] We might similarly split the difference for the paradox of sport, though nothing seems necessarily irrational about admiration for athletes unless it proves excessive, which it often does. As to why else sport should matter at all, and although there is a certain pluralistic arbitrariness at play, in explaining the potential (hyper) seriousness of games, perhaps Suits puts it best: saying that something 'is just a game is very much like saying to the Pope that Catholicism is just religion [or] to Beethoven that the quartets are just music' (1973: 64). As we saw in Chapter 5 with sport, fiction matters in part because of its symbolic potential. Sport fiction matters because sport does and because fiction does as well. What matters matters not merely in its actual instances, sport (or life) as it is but also in its *possible* instances, because these include sport (or life) as it *ought* to be, whether from an ethical, rational, or aesthetic point of view.

Notes

1 The anthology is by Whiting and Masterson (1974), the pertinent chapters Masterson (1974) on painting and Ghose (1974) on sports writing.
2 Examples include Holt and Pitter (2011) and Holt (2017).
3 I coin 'sportistic' here as convenient shorthand.
4 For a judiciously curated sample of such works, see Lowe (1977: 138–67).
5 Just as adduction, movement toward the midline, is the opposite of abduction, movement away from the midline.
6 See also Maes's account (2015: 315), which is similarly inclusive.
7 This line of argument is developed at greater length in Holt (forthcoming) to address the error card puzzle: if portraits must truly represent their subjects, how can error cards *mis*representing their subjects still count as portraits?

8 This is not necessarily so for other physical performances. For instance, Graham McFee argues (2011: 114) that watching broadcasts or recordings of dance performances is usually insufficient for having truly *seen* them, since they are meant to be experienced live in person.

9 Since Zidane is playing rather than posing, Freeland would exclude the documentary from the portrait class. But perhaps athletic portraiture should rather concern performance, or personality as *expressed* in performance.

10 Baseball lends itself to the sport fable subgenre in part because, as an E game in Kretchmar's sense (i.e., without time limits), it prompts a more contemplative mindset.

11 See Ramaeker (2014: 34) for a discussion of the interplay in the *Rocky* films between realistic drama and romanticized melodrama.

12 I define film noir as 'stylized crime realism' (2006: 25).

13 For more on the peak shift effect as applied to aesthetics, see Holt (2013: 4–5).

14 See for example Walton (2015: 75–6), who characterizes our engagement with both sport and fiction as kinds of make-believe.

15 Though this is not adequately addressed by extant scholarship, there are important differences between fictions *seen* and fictions *read*, in that unreflective basic emotions like fear are far more adaptive in response to visual stimuli than to textual stimuli.

References

Best, D. (1978) 'The Aesthetic in Sport', in *Philosophy and Human Movement*, London: George Allen & Unwin, pp. 99–122.

de Melo, V. A. (2012) 'Sharing (Modern) Experiences: Sport (Body) – (Image) Cinema', *Journal of the Philosophy of Sport*, 39 (2): 251–66.

Edgar, A. (2012) 'The Aesthetics of the Olympic Art Competitions', *Journal of the Philosophy of Sport*, 39 (2): 185–99.

Freeland, C. (2010) *Portraits and Persons: A Philosophical Inquiry*, Oxford: Oxford University Press.

Ghose, Z. (1974) 'The Language of Sports Reporting', in H. T. A. Whiting and D. W. Masterson (eds.) *Readings in the Aesthetics of Sport*, London: Lepus Books, pp. 57–68.

Holt, J. (2006) 'A Darker Shade: Realism in Neo-Noir', in M. T. Conard (ed.) *The Philosophy of Film Noir*, Lexington: University Press of Kentucky, pp. 23–40.

Holt, J. (2008) 'Terminator-Fear and the Paradox of Fiction', in S. M. Sanders (ed.) *The Philosophy of Science Fiction Film*, Lexington: University Press of Kentucky, pp. 135–49.

Holt, J. (2013) 'Neuroaesthetics and Philosophy', *SAGE Open*, 3 (3): 1–7.

Holt, J. (2017) 'The Philosopher's Stallone: Significance of the *Rocky IV* Training Montage', *Cinematic Codes Review*, 2 (1): 61–7.

Holt, J. (forthcoming) 'Sport Card Portraiture', in H. Maes (ed.) *Portraits and Philosophy*, New York: Routledge.

Holt, J. and Pitter, R. (2011) 'The Prostitution Trap of Elite Sport in *He Got Game*', in M. T. Conard (ed.) *The Philosophy of Spike Lee*, Lexington, KY: University Press of Kentucky, pp. 15–25.

Lamarque, P. (2003) 'Fiction', in J. Levinson (ed.) *Oxford Handbook of Aesthetics*, New York: Oxford University Press, pp. 377–91.

Lowe, B. (1976) 'Toward Scientific Analysis of the Beauty of Sport', *British Journal of Physical Education*, 7 (4): 12–8.

Lowe, B. (1977) *The Beauty of Sport: A Cross-Disciplinary Inquiry*, Englewood Cliffs: Prentice-Hall.

Maes, H. (2015) 'What Is a Portrait?', *British Journal of Aesthetics*, 55 (3): 303–22.

Masterson, D. W. (1974) 'Sport in Modern Painting', in H. T. A. Whiting and D. W. Masterson (eds.) *Readings in the Aesthetics of Sport*, London: Lepus Books, pp. 69–88.

McFee, G. (2011) *The Philosophical Aesthetics of Dance: Identity, Performance and Understanding*, Plymouth: Dance Books.

Ramaeker, P. (2014) 'Staying Alive: Stallone, Authorship and Contemporary Hollywood Aesthetics', in C. Holmlund (ed.) *The Ultimate Stallone Reader: Sylvester Stallone as Star, Icon, Auteur*, New York: Wallflower Press, pp. 27–52.

Spinicci, P. (2009) 'Portraits: Some Phenomenological Remarks', *Proceedings of the European Society for Aesthetics*, 1: 37–59.

Stear, N. -H. (2017) 'Sport, Make-Believe, and Volatile Attitudes', *Journal of Aesthetics and Art Criticism*, 75 (3): 275–88.

Suits, B. (1973) 'The Elements of Sport', in R. G. Osterhoudt (ed.) *The Philosophy of Sport: A Collection of Original Essays*, Springfield: Charles C. Thomas, pp. 48–64.

Walton, K. L. (2015) ' "It's Only a Game!": Sports as Fiction', in *In Other Shoes: Music, Metaphor, Empathy, Existence*, Oxford: Oxford University Press, pp. 75–83.

Whiting, H. T. A. and Masterson, D. W. (eds.) (1974) *Readings in the Aesthetics of Sport*, London: Lepus Books.

Wilberding, J. (2017) 'David Foster Wallace on Dumb Jocks and Athletic Genius', *Journal of the Philosophy of Sport*, 44 (1): 108–22.

9 Sport as art

The debate about whether sport can count as art is of long standing if not always of sustained interest. Diving into the literature, one soon gets a sense of immersion in a surprisingly viscous liquid through which it is exhausting to make any headway, much less achieve a breakthrough. This overall impression remains even in the face of fresh approaches that emerge from time to time in the literature.

Part of the problem is that art is a notoriously difficult subject to handle theoretically. Even assuming that art can be defined – a big if – or at least that certain conditions of inclusion and exclusion may simply be assumed, it is too easy to resolve this stubborn debate, as it were, by stipulation. If we understand the term 'art' to designate any domain of skilled activity, as in 'the art of living on a budget' or 'the art of winning friends and influencing people', and so on, then any sport – a game of physical skill – will trivially count as art, though this is not the sense in which we are interested in the question of whether sport can be art, that is, whether sport can be *fine* art. Suppose we cite Beardsley's aesthetic definition of art as 'an intentional arrangement of conditions for affording experiences of marked aesthetic character' (1979: 729, quoted in Arnold 1990: 181). Granting this definition straightforwardly implies that many sports count as art, since playing for aesthetic effect is a part of scoring in some sports and in others is frequently intended as desirable if unnecessary. On the other hand, if we assume that the beauty created in art must not be realized for some further end, that it may have no *transaesthetic* purpose, then sport will be, again trivially, excluded from the art class, since aesthetic effects will either be inessential or essential only as means to the end of scoring and winning.[1] Similarly, following David Best's curious life situations argument (1978: 115), if we stipulate that art must say something about life situations and that sport cannot do so, it naturally follows that sport cannot be art. Such stipulation is as vexingly arbitrary as it is convenient.

As we shall see, this is by no means the only way in which philosophers on either side of the sport-as-art debate tend to talk past one another. However, it does reflect the relative impasse at which the debate has seemed to stand for some time. Part of my purpose here is to reframe the debate so that the impasse can be overcome, giving both sides the due often denied them. I will argue that some sport performances count as art*works*, though fewer than is often supposed, and that figure skating (if no other sport) counts as an art*form*. A corollary of this view is that most sports are not artforms and most sport performances are not artworks. Where most philosophers begin with established sports and try to determine whether and how they may count as art, I also approach the question from the neglected other side by considering whether some art may count as sport, specifically artistic dance in competitive contexts.

Before we (re)frame the debate, it will be helpful to highlight certain essential distinctions and terms. First, we should mark the aesthetic/artistic distinction. Being beautiful or aesthetically pleasing is different from and insufficient for art. No one denies that sport can be beautiful, with certain elegant movements, graceful styles, and dramatic contests, for instance. These qualities may be associated with art, but they are also distinguishable from art, as a sunset and a painting of it may both be aesthetically pleasing although only one of them, the painting, is a work of art. Second, by art in this sense we mean individual works and general forms that count as fine art: painting, sculpture, poetry, theater, dance, music, and so on. If any sport counts as art, it will be something akin to theater or dance. Third, we should also note the beauty/aesthetic distinction in that something that would be totally unappealing in real life, such as an evil character, may well be aesthetically pleasing when depicted in an artwork. Hannibal Lecter may delight us in fiction but should not do so in real life. Fourth, we should note the aesthetic/purposive sport distinction: in aesthetic sports such as gymnastics, diving, and synchro, the scoring and outcome are at least partly determined by judged aesthetic criteria, whereas in purposive sports such as soccer, track, and weightlifting the aesthetic is at most a by-product, immaterial to competitive outcomes.

Framing the debate

One of the reasons the sport-as-art debate appears to be deadlocked, again, is that philosophers on either side appear to be talking past one another. Those naysayers who deny that sport is art tend to insist, for various reasons, that no sport counts as an art*form* (e.g., Best 1978; Cordner

1988; Hyland 1990; Mumford 2012; Allen 2013). As David Best suc-
cinctly puts it, 'I contend that *no* sport is an art *form*' (1980: 69, original and added emphasis).

Those who rather affirm the sport-as-art thesis,
however, tend to focus on insisting that certain sport performances count
as art*works* (e.g., Boxill 1985; Wertz 1985; Arnold 1990; Platchias 2003;
Elcombe 2010). As Peter Arnold articulates the point, 'a skater like Katarina Witt . . . embodies and articulates her aesthetic intent. . . . In her
rendering of the music from Bizet's *Carmen* at the 1988 Olympics she
was able to do this with perfection. . . . Similarly in the pair skating [*sic*]
of Torvill and Dean . . . skating to the music of Ravel's *Bolero*' (1990:
175).[2] Although the point of contention might not be entirely clear here,
it should be evident that there is a sharp division between hostile and
friendly attitudes toward the idea that sport is or can be art in some sense.

What might strike one, however, is the impression that critics and advocates of sport as art are focused on supporting positions that are neither
contrary nor contradictory but are rather entirely consistent. The naysayers might be right about artforms even if the proponents are right about
individual artworks. It might be the case *both* that no sport counts as an
artform *and* that certain sport performances count as artworks. This is
because questions about artforms concern *types*, which are logically distinct from questions about individual artworks: tokens rather than types.
Analogously, mental states may be token-identical to brain states – that is,
each one *is* a brain state – even if, for principled reasons, there is no single
type of physical state that corresponds to the mental type. More concretely,
note that Marcel Duchamp's *Fountain*, a urinal presented in a gallery, may
count as an artwork even though urinal presentation per se is not an artform. It may likewise be the case that figure skating, say, is not an artform
even if certain performances count as artworks. If one were to counter that
Fountain is an example of *objet trouvé*, or 'found art', which is an artform,
two replies are in order. First, *Fountain* was one of the first *objets trouvés*,
paving the way for – and thus not depending on – the established artform.
Second, even if the art status of certain skating performances required an
associated artform, just as *Fountain* stands in relation to found art, so too
would they stand in relation to the artform *dance*. If anything can be art,
that doesn't mean any type of thing can be an artform.

But the debate does not stop here. Both sides press further on the basis
of problematic if largely implicit assumptions. For naysayer Best, for
instance, figure skating as a sport will in *no instance* count as artwork
(1978: 121). This is in part because the activity of creating art is or is
supposed to be autotelic or aesthetico-telic, something done for its own

sake or the sake of aesthetic creation alone. Since the aesthetic is created in sport at most as a means to the desired end of scoring and winning, it is thereby not properly, since not purely, artistic. On the other side of the debate, a proponent like Boxill contends that a sport like basketball – indeed, sport generally – should be seen as an artform *because* great players like Dr. J and Kareem Abdul-Jabbar show great artistry in their unique, creative styles of play (1985: 36, 46).[3] In other words, the naysayers tend to be implicit *purists* about both sport and art, taking the view that no sport is an artform to imply that there is no case of sport performance that counts as an artwork, as well as seeing the creation of aesthetic beauty for some further end, like scoring or winning, to exclude the product from the art class. But just as such purism seems unwarranted, proponents tend to fall prey to undue *tokenism* by taking the view that some sport performances are artworks to imply that the sport itself is straightforwardly and unproblematically an artform. When made so explicit, neither the naysayer's purism nor the proponent's tokenism appears sufficiently plausible.

Since it is a matter of some dispute whether any individual sport performance counts as art, the best way to proceed, I think, is to replace the somewhat nebulous question 'Is sport art?' with the more focused 'Is sport *ever* art?' If sport is ever art, it will no doubt be so in the case of an aesthetic rather than purposive sport, and if any such sport is to count as an artform, doubtless it will be some such sport as figure skating. If figure skating as a sport ever counts as art, it will most plausibly be a performance such as Torvill and Dean's gold-medal 'Bolero' routine at the 1984 Sarajevo Olympics, a routine many consider to be one of the all-time high-water marks of figure skating artistry. Even Best, the most adamant naysayer of all, admits that figure skating is the most plausible case for sport as art, conceding even that it sometimes *does* count as art, albeit only in essentially noncompetitive (i.e., nonsport) contexts such as professional showcases where the purpose is entertainment, not winning (1978: 121). We can use 'Bolero' as a test case to determine first whether sport is ever art and then move to address the larger question of whether any sport is an artform.

The 'Bolero' burden

The naysayer's concession is a reasonable one. It is too implausible to deny that figure skating performances outside the competitive context of sport may constitute artworks. After all, figure skating is a peculiar kind of dance – dance on ice – and although some types of dance are nonartistic activities, dance is a bona fide artform. On the surface at least, the naysayer is perfectly consistent in affirming the arthood of skating outside the sport domain but denying the arthood of skating within the sport domain.

Problems arise, however, when we consider the possibility of particular routines being performed *both* in sporting and in noncompetitive contexts; Torvill and Dean have performed their 'Bolero' routine in noncompetitive showcases as well as in winning Olympic gold. The naysayer's position implies that this very same routine performed by the very same dance pair fails to qualify as art in the Olympics yet qualifies admirably in the showcase. We may assume for argument's sake that the aesthetic appeal of these several performances is similar, although the Olympic performance, because of the heightened tension of an event viewed by millions, is in reality a far more dramatic one. If the showcase 'Bolero' counts as art, the naysayer's burden is to explain why essentially the same performance, the Olympic 'Bolero', fails to count as art. If the 'Bolero' is showcase art, why not Olympic art as well?

It would be natural for the naysayer to answer this 'Bolero' burden by appealing to the landmark work on indiscernibles by Arthur Danto (1964). Part of Danto's insight is that what makes something an artwork is perceptually unavailable to an observer insofar as a pair of perceptually indistinguishable artifacts – such as one of Andy Warhol's *Brillo Boxes* and an ordinary carton of Brillo pads – may constitute art in the one case and non-art in the other. In a similar vein, the naysayer might claim that the Olympic 'Bolero', like the ordinary Brillo box, is not art, whereas the showcase 'Bolero', like a Warhol *Brillo Box*, is art. This insight has been a significant force in sculpting the profile of recent philosophy of art for decades now.

However, although this is a possible move by the naysayer, it is the wrong way to think of the Brillo box analogy. In the 'Bolero' cases it is not as though we have different agents with different performative intentions fashioning different works that happen to look the same; rather, we have the same performers doing the same beautiful routine with the same aesthetic intention: to represent a loving relationship, in rhythm with the music from Ravel, between two sometimes birdlike creatures in harmony with each other and ending with the beings' or their love's literal or metaphorical death. True, the Olympic 'Bolero' is intended to be aesthetically appealing for the sake of winning, just as the design of a normal Brillo box is meant to entice consumers. But it is more as if we have two Warhol *Brillo Boxes*: one in a gallery, one in a supermarket. Both count as art despite their different contexts and whether or not there are any transaesthetic purposes in play.

For the naysayer to insist, moreover, that the competitive context of sport is an *excluding* condition from the art class leads to the following reductio: that there can be no such thing as an art competition. This is because the minute an artist submits a work to be considered for some transaesthetic purpose – a sale, a critique, a competition – the naysayer's position implies that the art status of the work is thereby nullified, the 'proper' purpose of art being no more and no less than aesthetic creation itself. But this position is untenable or, at the very least, rather naive about the artworld. There *are* various permissible transaesthetic purposes for which art is made, among which we may count winning art competitions, and to deny this is too idealistic, somewhat naive about the motives of many artists for creating their works. So considered, the 'Bolero' test case shows that at least some sport performances, however few, also count as genuine artworks.

Dance as sport

Even if we could not show, as I believe I have, that some established sport also counts as art, that by itself would not close the debate, since it could turn out that some established art, in particular dance, in some cases might also count as sport. It is somewhat curious that philosophers of sport have effectively ignored this line of inquiry, although it should be noted that dance theorists have not been so neglectful. Guarino, for instance, maintains that as an art dance is not only sufficiently physically demanding to qualify as sport but also, no less important, that it is often sufficiently competitive to so qualify as well (2015: 77–8). I believe this line of argument is essentially correct. The art-to-sport inference seems at least as and perhaps more plausible than the sport-to-art inference, so it would behoove us to explore the art-as-sport angle of the sport-as-art question.

Backing up a bit, we should note that dance is not always an artform and comprises three different broad types: ceremonial dance of the sort we might find in a tribal ritual, social dance as happens for instance in nightclubs, and proper artistic dance such as ballet (Cohen 1962: 19). There may be some overlap among these categories. As I dance a foxtrot, it is barely even a social dance and certainly no artform, yet as Fred Astaire danced it, it is unquestionably art. Since not all dance qualifies as art, we must be careful to focus our question accordingly. The question is not whether dance *simpliciter* may count as sport but whether dance qua art may count as sport. Dance in a general unqualified sense fails to count as sport just as in a general unqualified sense dance fails to count as art. This is because sport is essentially a type of physical contest, whereas dance as an activity is not necessarily competitive.

But this does not settle the question of whether artistic dance in certain contexts qualifies as sport. Dance need not be artistic but is still an artform, and likewise artistic dance need not be competitive but still may qualify as sport, and even as a 'sportform', when it *is* competitive. We should distinguish at least two types of such competitive dance. First, there are types of artistic dance that are essentially competitive: competitive ballroom (i.e., so-called *dancesport*), b-boy battles, power cheerleading, and so forth. Then there are types of artistic dance that, though not inherently competitive, have significant, clearly defined competitive contexts. Take ballet. There are long-standing ballet competitions, such as the Prix de Lausanne, not to mention the inherently competitive nature of auditions, competing for roles and status within and among dance troupes, and so on. In both types of competitive artistic dance, the activity meets such a criterion of sport as "competitive events involving a variety of physical (usually in combination with other) skills, where the superior participant is judged to have exhibited those skills in a superior way" (Suits 1988: 2).[4] It is no accident that Sylvester Stallone, perhaps the quintessential sport film icon, directed the dance movie sequel *Staying Alive*. The opening scene is of John Travolta at a dance audition leaving it all on the stage to the music of Frank Stallone's 'Far from Over', a soundtrack that might just as well have accompanied an athlete at a walk-on tryout leaving it all on the field.

Setting aside the unfortunate, often implicit, and clearly problematic tendency to gender sport as 'masculine' and the arts as 'feminine', perhaps the strongest resistance to dance as sport is grounded in institutionalism. An institutional theory of sport requires that a sport not only be a game of physical skill but also have a 'wide and stable' following (Suits 1973: 59, 60). By this objection, although ballet has a wide and stable following, that is only in its noncompetitive artistic form; it lacks such a following in its competitive varieties. Likewise, dance activities like power cheerleading may be essentially competitive, but their followings also seem of insufficient standing for sport.[5]

In response to this naysayer's objection, the proponent has several plausible responses at the ready. First, we may object on principled grounds to an institutional requirement for sport (e.g., Meier 1988: 15–17). Second, we may note that institutional theories of *art* rather than sport do not require a wide and stable following for the activity type but rather artistic status conferral on, or public presentation of, the token: a criterion of art-works rather than artforms (Dickie 2000: 93, 96). Third, on the heels of this point, and returning to the sport-as-art question again, we may note that on the institutional theory of art a skater like Toller Cranston was perfectly able to make his competitive performances art, as he intended, by his own status conferral and public presentation. To object that the artworld and 'sportworld' are wholly disjoint institutions is simply a nonstarter. Fourth, we should note that at least some artistic dance competitions *do* have wide and stable followings, not only individual competitions like ballet's Prix de Lausanne (an international competition in its 45th year), but also artistic dance types like competitive ballroom. It is entirely fitting, not merely aspirational, to refer to competitive ballroom as *dancesport*.[6]

The artform question

Backing away from institutionalism, we may turn to considering what it means for a *practice* to count as an artform. Urinal presentation never became an artform, but the more general category of found art did become an artform, partly because of such groundbreaking works as Duchamp's *Fountain*. Intuitively, if somewhat sketchily, what makes something an artform is a combination of a sufficient number of artwork instances over-arched by a sufficiently robust creative practice. Thus *Fountain* helped inaugurate the artform of found art rather than urinal presentation. More traditionally, dance and painting are artforms because there are signifi-cant numbers of paintings and dances that count as artworks and because these works are embedded in sufficiently robust practices of creating such works. Their artform status is not undermined by the fact that not all paint-ing activities or dancings are artworks or by the possibility that such prac-tices might exist outside institutional contexts.

Very few sports meet such a criterion for artforms, but at least fig-ure skating does.[7] We should note that the failure of most sports to meet this criterion is at the heart of what makes the naysayer's position attrac-tive. Very few of the arts satisfy an analogous criterion for sportforms, but at least some competitive dance does. Even as a sport, figure skating is too similar to other forms of artistic dance not to be considered a variety thereof. Even as an art, competitive dance is too similar to other sport-forms not to be considered a variety thereof.

My conclusions, then, are that (1) some figure skating performances count as both sport and art; (2) some dance performances count as both art and sport; (3) figure skating (if no other sport) counts as an artform; (4) competitive dance (if no other sort) counts as a sportform.

Notes

1 See Mumford (2012: 41) for a succinct expression of this view.
2 Note that Torvill and Dean competed in ice dance, not pairs, and that if any sub-class of figure skating as sport also counts as art, ice dance is the most plausible given its particular constraints on jumps and so forth.
3 Boxill also highlights notable athletes from other sports (1985: 42).
4 It should be noted that this is Suits's mature view, in contrast to his earlier, game-centered, and explicitly institutional view (1973).
5 See for example Johnson and Sailors (2013: 270).
6 For a useful discussion of competitive ballroom as sport, see Marion (2008: Chapter 6).
7 Synchronized swimming might also qualify, though again the vast majority of sports will not.

References

Allen, B. (2013) 'Games of Sport, Works of Art, and the Striking Beauty of Asian Martial Arts', *Journal of the Philosophy of Sport*, *40* (2): 241–54.

Arnold, P. J. (1990) 'Sport, the Aesthetic and Art: Further Thoughts', *British Journal of Educational Studies*, *38* (2): 160–79.

Beardsley, M. C. (1979) 'In Defense of Aesthetic Value' (Presidential Address), *Proceedings of the American Philosophical Association*, *52* (6): 723–49.

Best, D. (1978) *Philosophy and Human Movement*, London: Allen & Unwin.

Best, D. (1980) 'Sport and Art', *Journal of Aesthetic Education*, *14* (2): 69–80.

Boxill, J. M. (1985) 'Beauty, Sport, and Gender', *Journal of the Philosophy of Sport*, *11* (1): 36–47.

Cohen, S. J. (1962) 'A Prolegomenon to an Aesthetics of Dance', *Journal of Aesthetics and Art Criticism*, *21* (1): 19–26.

Cordner, C. (1988) 'Differences Between Sport and Art', *Journal of the Philosophy of Sport*, *15* (1): 31–47.

Danto, A. (1964) 'The Artworld', *Journal of Philosophy*, *61* (19): 571–84.

Dickie, G. (2000) 'The Institutional Theory of Art', in N. Carroll (ed.) *Theories of Art Today*, Madison, WI: University of Wisconsin Press, pp. 93–108.

Elcombe, T. (2010) 'Is Ronaldo a Modern Picasso?', in T. Richards (ed.) *Soccer and Philosophy: Beautiful Thoughts on the Beautiful Game*, Chicago: Open Court, pp. 161–71.

Guarino, L. (2015) 'Is Dance a Sport? A Twenty-First-Century Debate', *Journal of Dance Education*, *15* (2): 77–80.

Hyland, D. (1990) *Philosophy of Sport*, New York: Paragon House.

Johnson, A. B. and Sailors, P. R. (2013) 'Don't Bring It on: The Case Against Cheerleading as a Collegiate Sport', *Journal of the Philosophy of Sport*, *40* (2): 255–27.

Marion, J. S. (2008) *Ballroom: Culture and Costume in Competitive Dance*, New York: Berg.

108 *Sport as art*

ng with Sport and Games', *Journal of the Philosophy of Sport*, 15 (1): 11–30.
Mumford, S. (2012) *Watching Sport: Aesthetics, Ethics and Emotion*, New York: Routledge.
Platchias, D. (2003) 'Sport Is Art', *European Journal of Sport Science*, 3 (4): 1–18.
Suits, B. (1973) 'The Elements of Sport', in R. G. Osterhoudt (ed.) *The Philosophy of Sport: A Collection of Original Essays*, Springfield: Charles C. Thomas, pp. 48–64.
Suits, B. (1988) 'Tricky Triad: Games, Play, and Sport', *Journal of the Philosophy of Sport*, 15 (1): 1–9.
Wertz, S. K. (1985) 'Sport and the Artistic', *Philosophy*, 60 (233): 392–3.

10 Dance as sport

In the preceding chapter we considered the possibility that some sport counts as art and that some art, namely competitive dance, counts as sport. In this chapter we will consider the latter possibility in greater detail, philosophizing about dance in earnest in the wider context of sportification, of what it means to make an activity, or some form of it, into a sport. This discussion will involve examining the different types of dance and delving into how philosophers have addressed dance as an artform.

First, though, it is worth observing that, relative to other artforms, philosophers of art for the most part have disregarded dance, as suggested by the provocative tile of an essay by Francis Sparshott, 'Why Philosophy Neglects the Dance' (1989). We might think that philosophy tends to neglect the dance because it is seen as a 'feminine' art and hence in a sexist culture is unduly relegated in importance. We might also think that it is because dance involves bodily movement not just as an instrument of artistic expression, as all the arts do, but essentially as the *medium* of such expression. Could it be that many aestheticians have been too cartesian in their outlook and thus denied or marginalized the importance of the body? Most sport philosophers will hardly be shocked by this suggestion. But Sparshott rejects both. He thinks that dance has simply failed to establish itself as an artform of major cultural significance: 'there has not yet been any available basis for a philosophy of dance. Nor can such a basis be invented by philosophers. Philosophers cannot invent or bestow seriousness; they can only explain it' (ibid.: 634). This might underrate dance's cultural cachet, but even if not, it may be that the very biases Sparshott dismisses might underlie what he sees as dance's lack of seriousness. In other words, Sparshott may be right that philosophers neglect dance not because *they* dismiss it as a feminine or bodily art but rather because the *culture* at large does, although, to be fair, history teaches us that philosophers may be guilty not only of inheriting the faults of their cultural environment but also of exacerbating and to a certain extent creating them.

Categorizing dance

As our next task we should establish an understanding of what dance is. (*Pace* Wittgensteinians, this will be offered merely as a *working* definition.) Noël Carroll provisionally defines dance as 'rhythmical bodily movement, often in concert with music' (2003: 583). This includes dance not only as an artform but in a broad sense. We should probably narrow this broad understanding of dance, since counterexamples come to mind of rhythmic body movement often accompanied by music that intuitively do not count as dance: sex and military marches. Excluding these from the dance class but still casting a wide net to cover artistic and non-artistic forms of dance, we might note that, unlike mime, which requires expressive movements of the face and hands, dance requires movements of the entire body. Theatrical acting usually involves expressive movement of the entire body, but those movements are not rhythmically structured as dance is even when it lacks musical accompaniment or, as in the case of tap, generates its own musical rhythms. Unlike a march or sexual congress, dance may be interpreted as a markedly expressive activity (not that military marches and sex are not expressive in *some* ways). Here, then, is my working definition: dance is expressive, rhythmically structured, full-body movement.

On such a conception, certain sport activities will unproblematically count as varieties of dance, for instance figure skating, synchronized swimming, and rhythmic gymnastics. However, since our working definition includes non-artistic along with artistic types of dance, that a sport counts as dance will not necessarily mean that it also achieves art status. Some may, but not just because they qualify as dance broadly conceived.

Here we should revisit Selma Jeanne Cohen's threefold distinction, briefly mentioned in the previous chapter, among types of dance: ritual, social, and theatrical, the latter being of most interest to philosophers of art (1962: 19). The ceremonies of ritual dance may include not simply those with practical functions, such as a rain dance, but also those that support or commemorate significant events, as with war dances. In this case the rhythmic full-body movement expresses something of the culture in which it occurs. Where the purpose of most social dancing is having fun, which we might call hedonic rather than cultural expression, particularly skilled examples, driven by different purposes, may elevate themselves into the realm of art, just as framing them in a competitive context helps establish them in the realm of sport. The latter is arguably true of theatrical dance as well, though in the first instance such dance is expressive in an artistic rather than communal or hedonic sense. We may also see skilled and elaborate ritual dances potentially bleeding into the art class or being appropriated for artistic dance.

What may not be entirely clear is how certain dancelike sports fit, or fail to, into Cohen's framework. Although, as I have argued, some figure skating may count as artistic dance, in other cases categorization is less obvious. Take synchronized swimming and rhythmic gymnastics. As both qualify as dance in a broad sense and exhibit some of the formal features of artistic dance, there is reason to think that their expressive potential, at least in their current form, falls short of the artistic range possible in figure skating. Only figure skating, for instance, exhibits a narrative potential similar to artistic dance (although admittedly figure skating programs provide vignettes in comparison with full-length ballets). Where, then, do synchro and rhythmic gymnastic fall? They seem neither artistic nor ritual nor social dances. Also, consider the thorny case of cheerleading. If sideline cheerleading fails to qualify as sport, it still qualifies as dance in a broad sense and as specifically ritual dance besides. But competitive cheerleading, which has a much more forceful claim to be counted as sport, is dislocated from the cultural expressiveness and ritual purpose of its sideline predecessor and so, like synchro and rhythmic gymnastics, doesn't fit clearly into any of Cohen's categories.

Does this mean that we should reject our working definition of dance? Not at all. Rather, we should supplement Cohen's original three categories with a fourth: competitive dance, whose bodily expression isn't primarily communal, hedonic, or artistic but *agonistic* (i.e., of an athletic contest). At its best, figure skating may blend agonistic and artistic expression perfectly, though most sports that count as dance will fall short of true artistry. Our main question, however, is not which sports count as dance but how dance may count as sport, and, since it is artistic dance that stands as the paradigm of dance generally, it is to dance as art that we now turn.

Dance as art

It would be pointless to attempt here a complete sketch of the philosophical aesthetics of dance. Nonetheless, there are several theoretical points – some foundational, some intriguing – relevant to our subsequent discussion. Both in general and specifically as an artform, dance is expressive, performable, and rhythmic. We will briefly alight on these points before considering how artistic dance and dance generally may become sportified.

We begin with the account of dance advanced by Monroe Beardsley, the most prominent advocate of what are sometimes called aesthetic theories of art, according to which artworks are aesthetic artifacts, those that do or are meant to provide for aesthetic experience.[1] It is clear why aesthetic theories would appeal to advocates of the sport-as-art thesis, since many performances in sport are intended to and actually do provide for aesthetic experience. Since Beardsley accepts the intentional version of aestheticism, which requires that a work be intended to arouse aesthetic response, one might reasonably expect him to define dance simply in terms of works using body movement or perhaps rhythmic body movement to provoke aesthetic response.

But Beardsley doesn't give such an easy a fortiori account of dance, because he wants to include non-artistic varieties of dance as well. For Beardsley, dance is not merely expressive but *excessively* so: 'If . . . there is more zest, vigor, fluency, expansiveness, or stateliness than appears necessary for [a pattern of movement's] practical purposes, there is an overflow or superfluity of expressiveness to mark it as belonging to its own domain of dance' (1982: 35). What transforms ordinary movement into dance, then, is a *superfluity* of expressiveness. This account is intuitive if we think of the difference between ordinary actions and the representation of such actions in a dance. When I put on a hat, that may be expressive, but when a dancer does so on stage there is a gestural, exaggerated, practically excessive quality since the action *is* not only a putting on of the hat but also a *gesture* that represents putting on a hat. It is a performative version of a movement that in real life typically lacks such a quality.

That, however, is where Beardsley's account gets into trouble. Carroll and Banes offer as counterexample the phenomenon of what they call task dances, which consist in the performance of certain practical tasks without the flourishes of traditional dance (1982: 38). The key example is Yvonne Rainer's *Room Service*, in which dancers move different mattresses and arrange them on stage in prescribed ways. There is an analogy here between the ordinary movements of these task dances and the artform of found or readymade art. Just as an ordinary pattern of movement, such as lugging and arranging a mattress, may be offered on stage as dance, so too may ordinary objects – so-called readymades – be presented as works of art in a gallery. They paradigm here is Marcel Duchamp's *Fountain*, a pseudonymously signed, repurposed urinal.

We might defend Beardsley here by arguing either that these examples don't really count as dance and so are not genuine counterexamples or that they actually can be accommodated by Beardsley's theory despite appearances to the contrary.[2] Though Beardsley himself did not reply to Carroll and Banes, we can speculate that he likely would have rejected task dances, as he was rather adamant about denying that Duchamp's *Fountain* was art (2002: 242–3). Beardsley in my view did himself a disservice to reject *Fountain*.[3] Analogously, the more plausible move is to try to accommodate task dances as genuine dances. One might be pessimistic about this prospect if, as Carroll and Banes point out, 'a piece like *Room Service* cannot, on the pain of pragmatic self-contradiction, employ a superfluity of expressiveness beyond the practical, if it is committed to disclosing the intelligence of ordinary, practical work movements' (1999: 8). But is there any sense in which, contra Carroll and Banes, the performance of such tasks may be interpreted as a superfluity of expressiveness without pragmatic self-contradiction?

I believe so. Presumably the pragmatic self-contradiction here would be that of asserting that merely performing some prescribed task is *also* somehow more than merely performing that task – that *mere* practical expression is also *more* than mere practical expression and is therefore superfluous. But consider saying 'I love you' to someone. This will be expressively superfluous if done in too grand a fashion or too dramatic a tone in the given context, for instance beseeching my wife on bended knee in impassioned voice over our morning coffee, which would often seem excessive, silly. However, even without a too grand or too impassioned tone, saying 'I love you' may constitute a superfluity of expressiveness if one says it too often or otherwise unnecessarily, that is, in contexts where it is not needed. So too with moving mattresses. When one moves to a new home, lugging the mattress is necessary and so will not count as a superfluity of expression. But lugging the same mattress in the same way as part of *Room Service*, though not superfluous in *manner* of movement, is nonetheless superfluous as a *gesture* insofar as the mattress does not need to be moved at all! It needs to be moved as part of the dance, of course, but, unlike moving into a new home, performing the dance itself lacks such practical necessity. In framing his original criterion for dance, Beardsley considers that 'If every motion of the Corn Dance is prescribed in detail by magical formulas or religious rules to foster germination, growth, or a fruitful harvest, we might best regard it [not as dance but] as pure ritual' (1982: 35). Displaced from the need for a fruitful harvest, though, the non-superfluity of such a ritual itself becomes superfluous. The upshot here is that Beardsley's criterion for dance might be preserved, though Carroll and Banes could insist that superfluous expression fails to imply superfluity of expressiveness. Perhaps it is only dance in a traditional sense that meets Beardsley's criterion, whereas *Room Service* and other erstwhile avant-garde dances ultimately count as expressive rather than superfluously so.

In any case, artistic dance is not only expressive; it is also *performable*. It is a performing art in which works created by choreographers are executed by dancers. Just as figure skaters can perform the same program on different occasions, so too dancers often execute the same work in multiple performances. What makes two different performances performances of a single work?

One standard answer is that different performances correspond to the same notational score, as in the case of musical performances, although, unlike music, dance practice seems less reliant on scoring and has a greater variety of notational systems (e.g., Labanotation, Benesh). This account originates with Nelson Goodman (1968) but has recently been much more elaborately developed by Graham McFee (2011). For McFee, the multiple performability of a dancework is something philosophy of dance needs to explain.

Much as it seems we should agree with McFee on this point – even originally improvised works may be reperformed subsequently – his view includes certain commitments that strike me as both counterintuitive and unnecessary. The first of these is that, since danceworks are created and it is the choreographers rather than the dancers who author them, 'dancers are not artists (to put it very bluntly)' (ibid.: 170). Since the artist role here is best identified as the choreographer, there is no need or room to consider the dancer a performing *artist* as much as raw material used by choreographers to realize their vision. The second problematic claim, as I see it, is that dance on film is not really dance. If someone experienced dance only by watching recordings, 'in most contexts, we should reject our person's claim to experience of dance' (ibid.: 114). Dance on film at most constitutes 'a new, hybrid art form' (ibid.: 110). Third is the commitment to a version of what aestheticians call 'intentionalism', the view that a work of art means what the artist intended it to mean. As McFee puts it, in standard cases 'one has a right to expect the artist's intentions to cohere with the [correct] understanding of his/her work' (ibid.: 126). Hence artists' intentions as manifest in their works are often our best guide to grasping the meaning of those works.[4]

The contentiousness of these commitments becomes starker when we consider dance in relation to other performing arts, music and theater in particular. If it is choreographers rather than dancers who are the artists in dance, this would seem to imply that in music it is composers rather than musicians and singers who are the artists, that in theater it is playwrights and perhaps directors rather than the actors. But to say that Cole Porter is an artist but not Frank Sinatra, that Shakespeare is but not Laurence Olivier, is not defensible. Especially in the performing arts, the label 'artist' attaches not only to those who create the recipes for performance (choreographers, composers, playwrights) but also to those who create performances from such recipes (dancers, musicians, actors). Likewise, if dance on film isn't really dance, we are not justified in asserting that Fred Astaire and Ginger Rogers were great dancers but can claim only that they were great practitioners of – no, raw materials for – some hybrid film-dance artform. So too it would seem to follow that acting on film is not really acting either, just a hybrid film-theater artform, which seems a clear reductio of the target view.[5] Finally, since dance and other artwork can manifest failed as well as successful intentions, a work's meaning is a better guide to the artist's intent than vice versa. Interpretation may be constrained by the perceptible features of works, but rewarding interpretations can differ from one another and artists' intentions alike.[6]

As a last point, consider that dance is not just an expressive and performable artform but also, as rhythmically structured, one that resembles not only music but, perhaps surprisingly, also poetry. The basic biological appeal of the rhythmic arts should not be underestimated, especially if Nietzsche is onto something when he asserts that '[a]fter all, aesthetics is nothing but a kind of applied physiology' (1976: 664).[7] The rhythmic kinship between dance and music has long been acknowledged. Indeed, although dance may proceed without musical accompaniment, it very seldom does. Music is all but indispensable to most dance practices. That shouldn't make us complacent, though, in assuming that music itself, and not just rhythmic structure, is required for dance or that the relationship between dance and music is straightforwardly that one dances *to* music. As Sparshott observes, the relationship proves far much more nuanced than that (1995: 223). One may dance not just *to* the music or *with* it but also *against* it, *between* it, *from* it – pick your preposition. Some dancers, indeed, prefer a non-prepositional locution: they don't dance to the music, they dance the music, as if the movements themselves were on a par with the notes of the score: dance as embodied music, perhaps. In my view, dance theory and practice alike would benefit remarkably by pivoting away from the ossified clichés of dance-in-relation-to-music and toward the open possibilities of dance-in-relation-to-poetry.[8] Theoretical exploration could at last give substance to the virtually empty if evocative phrase 'poetry in motion'.

The sportification question

In the previous chapter I suggested that sportifying dance requires that it be put in a competitive context. Bracketing the possibility of institutional requirements for sport as well for the moment, this may suggest that *any* activity could be sportified simply by making it into a competition (as with many reality TV programs). This impression is false. Some activities, however competitive they are and whatever institutional trappings they may have, cannot be sportified simply because they are not activities of the right *kind*. Consider the game of chess. Although chess is extremely competitive at high levels, it cannot qualify as sport because it is not a game of physical skill but rather a game of strategy. Sports may or may not involve strategy as a significant determiner of outcome, but they absolutely need to involve physical skill. Even though thinking is a physically realized process, merely strategic games do not test physical skill. Similarly, though more subtly, we can reject the notion that e-sports are sports since they demand fine motor control rather than gross physical skill and because they are realized in virtual domains rather than physical space.[9] Unlike chess and e-sports, since dance requires gross motor skill, it is a suitable candidate, in the right context at least, for sportification.

Dance is similar in this respect to the martial arts, another domain of gross physical skill that need not but also may be sportified. One source of resistance to this domain assimilation is Barry Allen, who argues that despite their similarities – incorporating aesthetically appealing body movements, being governed by conventions – dance, sport, and martial arts are inherently disjoint activities. According to Allen, whereas dance is symbolic (rather than useful) and sport skills are useful only within internal game frameworks, martial arts training is useful outside the dojo (2013: 249). Though this account has some plausibility when the domains are considered in their entirety, it loses strength when considering specific examples. Even if sport skills generally (as opposed to basic physiological capacities) by and large have little real-world usefulness, this is hardly the case with combat sports like boxing, which has a similar external practical value to that of martial arts. Similarly, figure skating has symbolic potential comparable to artistic dance, and martial arts kata can have symbolic and even narrative significance. Instead of insisting that these activities are wholly disjoint – for example, that 'Olympic judo is not a martial art' (ibid.: 247) – a more nuanced taxonomy appears to be motivated, one that allows the inclusion of sport versions of martial arts alongside other varieties.[10]

The same would seem to apply to dance, although we should concede that competition is closer to the heart of martial arts than it is to the heart of dance. However, this impression might be misleading, even setting aside noncompetitive martial arts practices. Not only are there many inherently competitive dance practices such as competitive ballroom (dancesport), b-boy battles, power cheerleading, and dance competitions generally, but also we should remember various sports that also qualify as dance if not necessarily as art: figure skating, synchronized swimming, rhythmic gymnastics, perhaps even some so-called artistic gymnastics such as the women's floor routine.[11] One objection to taking dance competitions to count as sport is the sense that many of these are less rigorously scored than judged sports and so open the door to excessively biased outcomes.[12] (I rejected the subjectivity concern about aesthetic sports in Chapter 7.) To the extent that this is true, it is an unfortunate, though at worst a contingent, matter. There is nothing *necessarily* more biased about judging prima facie dance competitions (which may also be sports) than prima facie sport competitions (which may also be dance). Whatever institutional frameworks are presumed to be lacking to sportify competitive dance is also a contingent matter.[13] Thus, some competitive dance may count as sport just as some rhythmically structured sports count as dance.

Despite the partial convergence that I affirm between dance and sport and between sport and art, there remains an underlying inherent tension between the artistic and athletic aspirations of dance or any other activity. There are two evident but opposite traps: the virtuosic athleticism that neglects aesthetic expressiveness and the expressiveness that neglects physical prowess for the sake of aestheticism. Some figure skating critics may cite a pair of Canadians as examples of these respective flaws: Elvis Stojko and Toller Cranston. Indeed, such a tension buttressed early arguments against the prospect of sport as art. What is at stake may not be entirely clear in dance aspiring to be art or sport, or art to be sport, or sport to be art. But the tension between sport and art is inclusive and potentially fruitful. The sport–art tension, as with opposing muscle groups, is less about conflict than complementarity, or so it is pretty to think.

Notes

1 For discussion of the importance of the distinction between what I call 'aesthetic actualism' and aesthetic intentionalism, see Holt (2010: 76–7).
2 These approaches are suggested in Scott (1997) and Scott (1999), respectively.
3 For more on how aesthetic theories can accommodate *Fountain* as art, see Holt (2010: 81–3).

4 This is different from Beardsley's intentional requirement for art. If art must be produced with the intention to *cause* aesthetic experience, that does not imply that it must *mean* what the artist intended. Indeed, Beardsley was a strong advocate of anti-intentionalist interpretation.

5 McFee doesn't acknowledge this potential problem but does assert a disanalogy between dance and music: 'Perhaps a person who has listened to all of Mozart's compositions on DVD [*sic*] has heard all of Mozart's music' (ibid.: 113).

6 For more on this view as applied to literary interpretation, see Holt (2002: 74–6).

7 In this regard, I have long been tempted by the hypothesis that my father's love of bossa nova is rooted in his congenital heart arrhythmia.

8 Sparshott rejects the analogy in part because he believes poetic meter inappropriate to structure dance (ibid.: 231) and seemingly arrhythmic dance, unlike its poetic counterpart free verse, to be implicitly rhythmic (ibid.: 234). As a poet myself, I would stress both that free verse is implicitly if less rigidly rhythmic no less than arrhythmic dance and that it may only seem unsuitable to structure dance because of its unconventionality in serving that function.

9 For more on this, see Holt (2016: 7–9).

10 For instance see Martínková and Parry's discussion of martial sports (2016: 154–5).

11 Women's floor, unlike men's, has accompanying music and so a better claim to dance status.

12 This concern was raised in class by a few students with dance competition experience.

13 Note that dancesport was included in the 2018 Youth Olympic Games. I thank Jim Parry for this example.

References

Allen, B. (2013) 'Games of Sport, Works of Art, and the Striking Beauty of Asian Martial Arts', *Journal of the Philosophy of Sport*, 40 (2): 241–54.

Beardsley, M. C. (1982) 'What Is Going on in a Dance?', *Dance Research Journal*, 15 (1): 31–6.

Beardsley, M. C. (2002) 'An Aesthetic Definition of Art', in T. E. Wartenberg (ed.) *The Nature of Art: An Anthology*, Orlando: Harcourt, pp. 236–46.

Carroll, N. (2003) 'Dance', in J. Levinson (ed.) *The Oxford Handbook of Aesthetics*, Oxford: Oxford University Press, pp. 583–93.

Carroll, N. and Banes, S. (1982) 'Working and Dancing: A Response to Monroe Beardsley's "What Is Going on in a Dance?" ', *Dance Research Journal*, 15 (1): 37–41.

Carroll, N. and Banes, S. (1999) 'Beardsley, Expression and Dance: A Reply to Gregory Scott', *Dance Research Journal*, 31 (2): 6–13.

Cohen, S. J. (1962) 'A Prolegomenon to an Aesthetics of Dance', *Journal of Aesthetics and Art Criticism*, 21 (1): 19–26.

Goodman, N. (1968) *Languages of Art: An Approach to a Theory of Symbols*, Indianapolis, MN: Hackett.

Holt, J. (2002) 'The Marginal Life of the Author', in W. Irwin (ed.) *The Death and Resurrection of the Author?* Westport, CT: Greenwood Press, pp. 65–78.

Holt, J. (2010) 'Providing for Aesthetic Experience', *Reason Papers, 32*: 75–91.

Holt, J. (2016) 'Virtual Domains for Sports and Games', *Sport, Ethics and Philosophy, 10* (1): 5–13.

Martínková, I. and Parry, J. (2016) 'Martial Categories: Clarification and Classification', *Journal of the Philosophy of Sport, 43* (1): 143–62.

McFee, G. (2011) *The Philosophical Aesthetics of Dance: Identity, Performance and Understanding*, Plymouth: Dance Books.

Nietzsche, F. (1976) 'Nietzsche Contra Wagner', in W. Kaufmann (ed. and trans.) *The Portable Nietzsche*, New York: Penguin, pp. 661–83.

Scott, G. (1997) 'Banes and Carroll on Defining Dance', *Dance Research Journal, 29* (1): 7–22.

Scott, G. (1999) 'Transcending the Beardsleyans: A Reply to Carroll and Banes', *Dance Research Journal, 31* (1): 12–9.

Sparshott, F. (1989) 'Why Philosophy Neglects the Dance', in G. Dickie, R. Sclafani, and R. Roblin (eds.) *Aesthetics: A Critical Anthology* (2nd Ed.), New York: St. Martin's Press, pp. 629–34.

Sparshott, F. (1995) *A Measured Pace: Toward a Philosophical Understanding of the Arts of Dance*, Toronto: University of Toronto Press.

Index

Note: Page numbers in *italics* indicate figures and those in **bold** indicate tables.

Printed in the United States
by Baker & Taylor Publisher Services